SiLeNCe is a sCary sound

And Other Stories on Living Through the Terrible Twos and Threes

Clint Edwards

author of *I'm Sorry . . . Love, Your Husband*

PAGE STREET
PUBLISHING CO.

PAGE STREET
PUBLISHING CO.

Copyright © 2019 Clint Edwards

First published in 2019 by
Page Street Publishing Co.
27 Congress Street, Suite 105
Salem, MA 01970
www.pagestreetpublishing.com

Distributed by Macmillan, sales in Canada by The Canadian Manda Group.

23   22   21   20   19   1   2   3   4   5

ISBN-13: 978-1-62414-853-8
ISBN-10: 1-62414-8530

Library of Congress Control Number: 2019931580

Design by Meg Baskis for Page Street Publishing Co.
Cover Image: Shutterstock/CSA-Printstock

Printed and bound in the United States

"Clint brings wit and wisdom to his writing that is a must-read for every parent."

-Love What Matters

"HILARIOUS!!"

-Tiffany Jenkins, the viral mother behind Juggling the Jenkins

"This book is so funny you might pee a little. Ok, maybe a lot . . ."

-Meredith Ethington, Filter Free Parents

"Clint just gets it. I love to laugh and he NEVER disappoints."

-Meredith Masony, the viral mother behind That's Inappropriate

"Hilarious and all too true!"

-Brian Gordon, Fowl Language Comics

What other people are saying about Clint Edwards

"Amen!"

-Parents Magazine

"Clint Edwards brings real humor to the unsavory parts of childcare . . ."

-Mashable

"I always know, when I'm about to read a piece by Clint, that I'll end up nodding my head in agreement . . ."

-The Washington Post

For Tristan, Norah, and Aspen

You are the reason for, and the reason
I regret, my vasectomy.

Contents

The Terrible Twos   21
(Cue *Jaws* Theme Song)

The Threenager 187

"A two-year-old is kind of like having a blender, but you don't have a top for it."

-Jerry Seinfeld

They Start to Walk and Your Life Begins to End

―――――――――――― ― ― ― ― ―

My favorite time as a parent was that sweet spot where our baby could sit up but not crawl, or walk, or talk. I could put him in one place. He couldn't run away, he couldn't get into mischief, and he couldn't talk back. As long as I gave the child a few things he could safely stick in his mouth, he was good for hours. But then he started to move, jabber on, and boom! My life was over.

Was that too harsh?

Perhaps there's a better way to phrase it?

Thinking.

Thinking.

Nope, sorry.

You're screwed.

The moment a child begins to walk, your life begins to end. And once they can turn on the TV in the morning, your life begins again. But right there, in the heart of it all, are the twos, threes, and fours—and they are exhausting, and confusing, and hilarious, and this book is one father trying to make sense of it all. It's a collection of essays, lists, epiphanies, exaggerations, and lunatic ramblings from a father of three laughing at a train wreck. Oh . . . and poop. There's also a lot of poop in here. But honestly, how could I write a book about toddlers without it? If all the toddlers in the world were artists, poop would be their medium.

Mel and I have been married since 2004, and we have three children, Tristan, Norah, and Aspen. Not to state the obvious, but they were all two, three, and four once. And it sucked. Each and every time it sucked. It sucked bad, in ways that I didn't know sucking could suck so much. (I'm sorry, that was a lot of "sucks" used in one sentence, but I wasn't aware of another word that fits life with a toddler better than "sucks.")

Okay, hold on. This introduction is going off the rails a bit. Let's get back on track, because honestly, my goal with this book is to bring you hope.

I'm all about hope when it comes to raising children.

I've been spreading hope online for years. I'm the author of the popular and hilarious daddy blog No Idea What I'm Doing, and I'm a staff writer for the very awesome Scary Mommy. I've written about parenting for the *New York Times*, the *Washington Post*, the *Huffington Post*, and a bazillion other publications. My breakout hit, *I'm Sorry . . . Love, Your Husband*, made a pregnant woman laugh so hard she went into labor (this is not an exaggeration; she sent me a Facebook message about it). In fact, some of the chapters in this book were inspired by work I published on my blog and other places I've published my writing. This is one of the things I like the most about writing books. I get the opportunity to add all those details I always wanted to in the original but that would have made it too long for an online post. (The internet . . . ain't nobody got time for more than a thousand words.) So if you see something you recognize, that's cool. You probably read it online. But keep reading, because it's only going to get better.

Trust me.

My breakout hit, I'm Sorry . . . Love, Your Husband, made a pregnant woman laugh so hard she went into labor (this is not an exaggeration; she sent me a Facebook message about it).

This book will make you feel so much better about living with a toddler.

How do I know this?

Because I'm happy to announce that I am

done with the toddler years. I don't say this to make those of you in the throes of managing a booger-eating, two-foot-tall gangster with a passion for taking off their pants feel bad. I say it because: I survived and you will too.

Don't roll your eyes.

You will laugh again.

Probably while reading this book.

Hopefully.

(My wife thinks I'm funny . . .)

For me, the toddler years were nonstop chaos with short, tender moments where I'd hope that my child was appreciating me.

At least, I assumed as much because he gave me a sweet smile, or a soft touch, or perhaps he threw up on the tile instead of the carpet, which, I'm sorry, actually feels like a sweet sentiment when you're in the thick of it.

For me, the toddler years were nonstop chaos with short, tender moments where I'd hope that my child was appreciating me.

That's how much toddlers lower your standards.

I can still recall the moment my oldest first used the potty. He'd just turned three. I was standing over him in the restroom. He sat there with his little legs dangling seven inches above the floor, *Toy Story* underwear around his ankles. He looked up at me with the softest, sweetest little smile that seemed to say, "Thank you." Or at least that's what I told myself it said. It helps to make assumptions that make it appear like your toddler appreciates all your hard work.

I must admit, though, in all seriousness, I felt a huge sense of satisfaction in that moment, like I'd really shown my son something important, because . . . I had.

As a father of toddlers, I spent so much time asking, "Why?"

Little victories like that make it all worth it.

But now, looking back, I can say that in the moment, those victories were maddening, but they really weren't that horrible. Sure, toddlers are frustrating, loud little humans with a lot of developmental issues, and poop issues, and body fluid issues (frankly, all their valves are bad), but it's the reality of accepting that they are developing that will make this whole endeavor a little more bearable.

And I get it—you might actually be trying to read this book with a snot-nosed slimy human attached to your leg, a twenty-pound wet diaper resting on your comfort shoes (probably Crocs), boogers on your yoga pants.

But it's true.

As a father of toddlers, I spent so much time asking, "Why?" Why did my child take their shoes off in the men's room? Why did they try to eat dog poop? Why won't they let me pee alone? But eventually, I started to accept that what I was dealing with was a very, very, raw product. I abandoned logic and accepted, in the core of my being, that my young child was just trying to figure *everything* out. And it was only then that I stopped wanting to light the house on fire.

We are all failing at this toddler gig.

You.

Me.

Even the mother who actually gets dressed nice to go grocery shopping.

Is this making you feel better?

Probably not.

Chances are you bought this book in the hopes of finding some sort of tip or trick to make life easier, but I'm sorry, you won't find that here.

But wait! Don't shut the book yet.

Please!

Let me finish.

What you will get is an account of what it's like to live with a toddler. The reality of it. The gritty, sticky, frustrating truth. Much of what I've said so far sounds dismal, sure, but it's not nearly as dismal as all those parenting books that give you tips that don't work and ultimately make you feel like a parenting failure. You don't need that in your life. What you need is support. You need group therapy. You need to laugh at it all and realize it's not just you.

We are all failing at this toddler gig.

You.

Me.

Even the mother who actually gets dressed nice to go grocery shopping. Even her, with her flawless Instagram account and sweet-smelling dry-shampooed hair. She's losing her mind too. She's had to pull the car seat onto the lawn and hit it with the garden hose, same as you. What I want you, my awesome reader, to get from this book is that raising little ones is the first step to failure. And you know what? That's okay. There's no winning here. Regardless of education, income, status, race, religion, nationality, we are all losers elbow-deep in our toddlers' poop.

So much poop . . .

Toddlers are the great equalizers.

So sit down and embrace it.

No shame.

The Terrible Twos

(Cue *Jaws* Theme Song)

That Time My Two-Year-Old Hit an Old Lady in the Face with a Snake

———————

I carried my son, Tristan, on my shoulders into church, his left hand holding on to my forehead for balance, the other cradling a collection of rubber snakes. He wasn't into *real* snakes. He didn't want a pet snake or anything. He didn't approach random snakes, pick them up, and show them to his mother like some little boys do. He wasn't even into seeing snakes at the zoo. But rubber snakes, for whatever reason, really appealed to him, and I think it had to do with how stretchy they were.

Mel was very pregnant at the time—ready-to-pop, waddling pregnant. She wore a long green maternity dress, her feet swollen, her shoes all stretched out. We'd reached that stage where Mel picking up Tristan wasn't all that easy, so although it'd never been discussed formally, it was obvious that I was on toddler duty.

Mel sat down on a bench, and I took Tristan off my shoulders and set him down on the blue church carpet with his snakes. Five, ten, fifteen, I can't recall exactly how many snakes he had. But what I do remember was that his arms were full of them, a mix of neon and earth colors, all made from rubber.

Back then, I'll admit, I was pretty over the snakes. I didn't like the way he swung them over his head like a lasso, knocking things off shelves and almost smacking himself in the face. I didn't enjoy the way he liked to stretch one as far as his little chubby toddler arms could reach, his face getting all red, grunting, and then letting it go to see how far it would shoot across the room, often smacking me or my wife or landing in the casserole. Once he rubbed a snake down with applesauce and then dragged it across the living room, making slithering snake sounds and ruining the carpet. Sometimes he put them in his pants— four or five of them—one snake hanging from the side of his shorts like a . . . well, you get the idea. Then he'd prance around the house, working his hips, doing his "snake dance."

And I really didn't like that, regardless of how many times we told Grandma not to buy Tristan toy snakes, he almost always came home with a new snake after visiting her home. She'd insist that it was just one more, and he really wanted it, and hey, what are grandmas for . . . right?

Not to say that Mel and I were any better about not giving in to our son's rubber snake demands. One day, for example, he stretched out a massive black and green python-looking thing, let it go, and smacked me right in the crotch. Right in the money zone. I took the snakes away, he cried, he threw a fit, and eventually, I gave them back. He shoved one in the toilet, flushed it, and we had to call a plumber to get it out. We took away the snakes for a few days, but eventually we gave them back. It was a perpetual cycle, really.

And I started to wonder if the experts who write books about boundaries with toddlers have ever actually *lived* with a toddler.

Were we bad parents? You know, if I take a look at any parenting book on raising a toddler, I'm sure it will tell me we were not setting clear boundaries. We were creating a cycle of fits and only making our lives worse. We needed to dig in our heels and bury those snakes in the yard like they were weapons of mass destruction. I read stuff like that before becoming a parent, and I bought into it. Then, when it went from theory to practice and I was actually living with a toddler, I started to realize that it isn't as much about boundaries as it is about sanity. And I started to wonder if the experts who write books about boundaries with toddlers have ever actually *lived* with a toddler. Because I could set boundaries all day, and the moment I got done establishing them, my kids would find some other way to make me want to run into the woods and live, alone, toddler-less.

All of it felt like I was raising Voldemort, but at the time, I was comfortable with that as long as it meant passing my midterms.

As much as I hated those rubber snakes, I was still in college. I needed them in my life as much as Tristan did—because when he had his snakes, he'd be quiet. He'd play with them for hours, focused 100 percent on stretching them. On whispering to them. On building them little snake villages with pillows and blocks and trucks. When he had his snakes, I could load the dishwasher, or fold some laundry, or read a textbook without him clawing at me for attention. All of it felt like I was raising Voldemort, but at the time, I was comfortable with that as long as it meant passing my midterms.

And on Sunday, if Tristan had his snakes, he'd sit through at least 50 percent of church without running to the pulpit with me chasing him in a collared shirt and tie and catching him moments before he snagged one of the microphones and screamed, "Snakes!" He wouldn't try to rip the pages out of the hymn books, or draw on the benches, or scream for snacks, or suck milk from his sippy cup and spit it on the floor to create a puddle he could jump in.

And I know that 50 percent doesn't sound like much, but we're Mormons, so that means we attend church for three hours (I kid you not). With enough snakes and a sandwich bag of Teddy Grahams, I could take the sacrament, get a prayer or two in, and maybe even participate in a lesson without having to wander the halls of the chapel with my little boy, his white shirt and tie soaking wet, his face red from crying because I wouldn't let him perform his own baptism in the drinking fountain.

So we went to church that Sunday, just weeks before Mel was to give birth, our son on the floor and surrounded by rubber snakes, a cobra in one hand and a sandwich bag of Teddy Grahams in the other, all of it looking like he were some sort of sacrifice. Mel had her right hand on her stomach, her hips moving in the bench, obviously uncomfortable.

The chapel was long with white walls, a vaulted ceiling, and old wooden benches with blue upholstery that matched the carpet. At the front was a dark wood podium. We were in Provo, Utah, so the place was packed with other Mormons. One member said the opening prayer. I lowered my head and closed my eyes, which, I will admit, was a bad call. Not that praying is bad. I'm down with that. It was more the act of taking both eyes off my toddler. When I think back on this moment, I realize that I assumed the Lord would have my back. That as I was praying, dutifully, giving him praise for all his generous blessings, that he'd keep an eye on my son. Perhaps put him to sleep or just place him in some sort of religious trance. But as it turns out, God doesn't work that way and neither do toddlers.

I'm not sure if there's a moral lesson to learn here. I'm not sure what the religious significance is of my toddler getting into mischief, even as I'm praying. Does this prove that God doesn't exist? Does it prove that toddlers are actually the devil? I don't know, but frankly I tend to lean toward the latter. I peeked through one eye to see Tristan stretch his rubber cobra out as far as he could—and let it snap. It sailed high into the air, almost struck the vaulted ceiling, passed the hanging light fixture, and came crashing into the face of an elderly woman, who, I might add, had her eyes shut, luckily, or she'd have probably lost one of them.

I'm not sure what the religious significance is of my toddler getting into mischief, even as I'm praying. Does this prove that God doesn't exist? Does it prove that toddlers are actually the devil?

She was wearing a yellow dress that had seen a few too many wash cycles, a red brooch pinned to her chest, her hair in a gray dome of curls. I didn't know her, just knew of her. She was the aunt of a friend of mine. She rubbed her face and then looked down. I was swimming in a mix of emotions: embarrassment, frustration, anger. But I must say, looking back now, I cannot help but laugh because that woman picked up Tristan's toy cobra as if God himself had struck her with it.

Then the prayer ended. Tristan had a confused look of wonderment that seemed to say, "I didn't think it would shoot that far." Once he looked at me, though, it all changed to absolute terror because he knew he'd done something wrong but wasn't quite sure what. Two-year-olds are like that. They almost have a sense of right and wrong, but it seems to kick in only after they've actually done the wrong thing. It's pretty frustrating, and it took me years of hard work to get each of my children to understand that they can stop bad things from happening by not actually doing them.

> I cannot help but laugh because that woman picked up Tristan's toy cobra as if God himself had struck her with it.

As a responsible father, I knew I had to do something, and yet how could I explain this? A few years ago I came across a headline that read "Wife Stabs Husband with Squirrel." Turns out it was a ceramic squirrel, but nevertheless, I remember wondering how she explained this to the cops. Did she apologize to her husband? And what did that look like? Did she lean across the court bench and say, "I stabbed my husband with a squirrel. I deeply regret my actions. Please forgive me"? How did she find the words?

I felt similarly as I approached that elderly lady, her face a little red from being struck by a rubber cobra. I sheepishly walked across the chapel, came up behind her, and, despite all the wholesome advice I'd received before becoming a father, did something no one ever prepared me for. This is the reality of a toddler. They often defy explanation or logic, and suddenly you find yourself leaning across a church bench, whispering into an elderly woman's ear, "I'm sorry my son hit you in the face with a snake. Are you hurt?"

She wasn't, luckily.

And legally.

I'm not sure what the lawsuit would've looked like over my toddler hitting her with a rubber snake. She did give me one of those knowing smiles that come from someone who's been there with a toddler as she handed back the cobra.

Then she patted my hand and winked.

I took Tristan outside after that. He followed me, one hand cupped in the other, fearful. Cradled in my arms were all of his snakes. By this point, I was angry. I was embarrassed. I was a lot of things, and the one emotion that united them was my desire to throw all his snakes in the garbage. We stood out in the hallway, and he looked up at me with these big, blue, sad, watery eyes. He'd been here before. He knew what I was planning.

Tristan could say a few words like "yes" and "no." (He said "no" a lot.) He could also say "thank you," and "please," and "snakes." He could say "cat" but not "dog" or "horse" or "cow," making every four-legged animal he saw a "cat." As I leaned down to his level, snakes in my hands to give him a lecture, he said, "Sorry" before I could get a word out. I'd never heard that word from him before. I wasn't even sure if he knew exactly what it meant, but as he looked down at the carpet, I realized he probably did.

Then the craziest thing happened. It was something that seems to happen a lot with toddlers . . . all that anger I was feeling washed away. I don't know how they do it. I don't know how they can take a steaming-hot embarrassing moment, and with one gesture, one tucked lip, one word, make it all melt down into a warm heart— but there I was, moments earlier ready to burn all the snakes, and he flipped it on me.

I let out a breath. I thought for a moment. I knew this was a big leap for him, and I didn't want to stifle it. And part of me was, well, proud of him for learning the art of remorse. So I went another direction. I told him that I was disappointed, but I was proud of him for saying sorry. I told him I was going to throw the snakes away, but now I'm only going to take them away for a few days. But he could keep one of them. With a two-year-old it's difficult to determine how much they are actually taking in. Part of me always assumed he wasn't listening and that was usually when he picked up something, like the word "douchebag."

But, in that church hallway, I had a feeling that he was learning more than I realized. I held out his snakes and let him pick one—naturally, he grabbed the cobra.

Well played, I thought. *Well played.*

I took the rest of the snakes out to the car. Then we went back to the church bench and he sat on my lap quietly, hugging his snake.

The Pediatrician Won't Do Jack
(but That Isn't the Point)

———————

Tristan had been throwing up for about twelve hours. This was one week before his second birthday. He didn't have anything left but dry heaves. Mel and I were still young and poor and without good insurance, and although Tristan was obviously sick (I'd used the carpet cleaner relentlessly in those twelve hours, cleaning everything from the carpet to the sofa to myself), I didn't want to take him to the doctor because I knew, with 100 percent certainty, that they wouldn't do anything until he was two.

How did I know this? Because in the past two years we'd taken Tristan to the doctor about eight hundred bazillion times. Is that an exaggeration? Perhaps it was more like eighty times? You know what, it doesn't matter how many times exactly—it was a lot. At each visit, the doctor checked his ears, looked down his little sore throat, looked in his eyes, tickled him, and then—*bam!*—stuck us with a massive bill. Sometimes the doctor would say something like, "Well, if he were two, I'd open the heavens and bless your child with health and safety, but since he's only one and a half, here's a bill for a million dollars because I'm useless in this situation, but my time is valuable."

And naturally, I went to the doctor. And they didn't do jack, and I ended up with a bill I couldn't afford.

Okay, okay. I'm sorry, that was another exaggeration. But in the heat of the moment, when I was so tired and my child was so sick, and he couldn't talk, only cry, and all he wanted to do was hug me, and each boogery puke hug felt like when Jabba the Hutt tried to hug Princess Leia in *Return of the Jedi*, I couldn't help but want something, someone, to fix it. And naturally, I went to the doctor. And they didn't do jack, and I ended up with a bill I couldn't afford.

Sometimes I imagined running into my doctor's office on Tristan's second birthday, holding the little guy in the air like he was some sort of a sacred sun god, and screaming, "He's two now! Do you hear me? Two! Give me all your cures. All your medicine. We are ready! He has come of age!"

Our insurance was through the university where I was a student. I can't remember the exact details on deductibles, but what I do remember was that our insurance after having our first child felt a lot like saying thank you to someone after they karate kicked your face. We were still paying bills from bringing the child into the world, as well as other bills that had to do with keeping him in the world, making all of it an endless cycle of bills. I wasn't interested in being rich, per se—I simply longed to live the kind of life in which I didn't have to get every scrap of toothpaste out of the tube and pack my lunches in recycled cottage cheese containers.

So, when Mel looked at me with fearful eyes and said, "We really should take Tristan to the doctor," I thought about how his birthday wasn't for another week and replied, "No. They won't do jack and we can't afford it."

It was just after 8:00 p.m. Tristan was white-faced and listless, wearing black and red dump truck–print footie pajamas. Mel had him on her hip. She wore faded jeans with holes in the knees (her hardware-store work pants) and a light green, off-brand Target store polo. Her hair was in a loose braid, and as we spoke, Tristan tried to throw up, but nothing came out.

"Look at him," she said. Her voice was hollow and fearful, eyes watery. She looked at me like our son was about to die. And hey, with a child that young, that was a real fear. But I felt so burned by doctors, and I was so flustered by the bills that seemed endless, that I dug in my heels a little more. I told her that he was fine. That he'd get over it. There was no reason to go running off to the urgent care after hours.

At one point, we looked up his symptoms on WebMD (rookie move, I know) only to be told that he had illnesses ranging from food poisoning to gastric adenocarcinoma (gastric cancer).

And as we argued, Mel gave me a cold, flat-lipped look, eyes narrow, shoulders rigid, as though I were placing her child in danger. At one point, we looked up his symptoms on WebMD (rookie move, I know) only to be told that he had illnesses ranging from food poisoning to gastric adenocarcinoma (gastric cancer) and that he needed to see a doctor immediately.

"I'm taking him," Mel said. "You can come if you want, I don't care. But we are going."

She paused for a moment, about to say something more, but stopped speaking and just looked at me. It was her eyes that said it all: "Cheap," "heartless," "dickhead" . . . "Cheap-heartless-dickhead." There were a number of mean names rolling around in her skull, but instead of spitting them out, she snagged her keys from the counter of our small two-bedroom farmhouse in rural Provo, Utah, and went out the back door, slamming it for good measure.

I sat on the sofa for a moment, fuming.

It wasn't until she started the car and put it in reverse that I went out to accompany her and Tristan to the doctor. I felt like it was my duty to come along, or at least that's what I told myself— deep down, I knew it had more to do with the "I told you so" factor. I was still young enough, and it was still early enough in our marriage, to think that saying, "I told you so" was a valid argument that would ultimately change something. It took me a number of years to realize that saying "I told you so," regardless of the situation, was actually a jerk thing to do (and also a wonderful way to earn a one- to five-night stay on the sofa).

I went to get in our small green Mazda Protege, Tristan strapped into the car seat, and Mel started to pull away. I actually had to jump into the car as it was moving.

"You could've killed me!" I said.

She slammed on the brakes and gave me these cold, dead eyes that seemed to say, "I wish I had."

Then she said, "I'm sure the doctor would've done more than 'jack' for you," taking her hands off the wheel to make air quotes.

I don't like to state the obvious, but she was pissed.

I say that because I don't want you to think I'm a complete idiot. But I was angry too. I understood why I was mad. I didn't want to waste more money on doctor visits. And I'd discussed my concern for our ever-growing medical bills with Mel previously, and how there was no need to take our child to the doctor before he was two because they wouldn't do anything. She always acted like I wasn't getting it. But what "it" was I couldn't seem to understand. I mean, what could be more black-and-white than being stuck with medical bills we couldn't afford?

I assumed Mel was on my side when it came to the budget, and for the most part we were a pretty good team there. We discussed the numbers together (we still do). But when it came to taking the kid to the doctor, it felt like we were pouring cash on a fire in hopes of putting it out, and I couldn't for the life of me understand why she'd want to do that.

We didn't speak the whole way to the urgent care. We didn't speak as we waited more than an hour in the waiting room, Tristan nuzzled into Mel's shoulder, pushing away from her every so often to dry heave. We didn't speak as they called us back, and we didn't speak as the doctor, a slender white man in his late thirties with receding red hair, went through the usual motions of checking our son's eyes, ears, and mouth.

He asked questions about when Tristan last ate and drank. Asked if he had wet diapers. Then he looked at his chart, and said, "Oh . . . he isn't two yet."

Mel and I made eye contact, and I gave her a smug "I told you so" half-grin.

She looked back at me with cold-blooded murder in her eyes.

"I'll admit, though, he does seem dehydrated. That can be dangerous at his age."

Mel broke eye contact when the doctor said that. She looked at him with tight-lipped fear and it reminded me that Mel was still a new mother. We'd only been at this parenting thing a couple of years, and while I hated the thought of losing a child, it was nowhere near the way Mel dreaded it. I think it kept her up at night, and a doctor saying something as simple as "that can be dangerous at his age" sat in her gut like a ten-pound stone.

She wasn't interested in medication, or cost, or any of that. She was interested in peace of mind.

The way she held Tristan tighter, the way her eyes got misty, the way her toes curled in her shoes, everything about her said fear.

Then the doctor looked a little more at the chart and said, "Well, his birthday is close enough. Let's get him something that will help keep some fluids down." He patted Tristan's round auburn head, and as the doctor began to write a prescription, Mel relaxed. It was a soft, smooth look of relief that I didn't fully understand, but when I think back, I realize that although doctors wouldn't do much for our child before he was two, that wasn't the reason Mel wanted to take him to the doctor. She wasn't interested in medication, or cost, or any of that. She was interested in peace of mind.

It was late as we drove to the pharmacy and left with some dissolvable tablets and off-brand, orange-flavored Pedialyte. We drove home, and Tristan drank and ate some, and kept it down. And once he was asleep in his crib, well after midnight, and Mel and I stood over him, watching him sleep, I said, "Okay. I get it now."

She reached out, took my hand, and gave it a squeeze.

Poop Doesn't Go Easily Down a Tub Drain

I was leaning over Aspen, my two-year-old, as she took a bath. She grunted a little, her face red, and pooped. Then she gave me a two-teeth, gummy smile, and "laughed."

It wasn't a "You're a sucker" laugh or an evil villain laugh, but more of the crazy, maddening laugh that only two-year-olds have, where they place their hands on their little round stomachs and point and laugh at nothing as if it's something. Only this time, it was something. It was poop, which floated to the top of the tub and then rolled over like a small dead fish, all brown and nasty.

I was home alone with Aspen, who, moments earlier, found a lost sippy cup behind the living room glider. She drank some curdled milk right before I picked her up over my head and tickled her. She was in footed pajamas with little pink bears on them, an outfit we got at Costco. Her blonde hair was mashed on one side from playing on the couch. She laughed, her blue eyes wide, and smiled—then she puked in my face.

It got in my mouth.

This wasn't the first time something like this had happened.

Or the last . . .

I know that if you're a nonparent reading this, your stomach just turned, and I understand. Before I had kids, a moment like this would've been a deal breaker. But now, after living through three toddlers, I know this could simply be any given Tuesday.

They really lower your standards.

If you make it through raising a two-year-old without ever getting pee, boogers, or puke in your mouth, you must have been deployed or wrapped in plastic.

Mel and I often joked about how our two-year-old's valves were bad. They were always leaking or stinking, and it was always our job to handle it. If you make it through raising a two-year-old without ever getting pee, boogers, or puke in your mouth, you must have been deployed or wrapped in plastic.

As a father of three, I've smelled some things.

Some really bad, nasty, could-be-placed-on-a-war-head-and-turned-into-a-chemical-weapon things. But this particular milk experience was in my top three of all nasties. It smelled like a cross between burning rubber, stomach acid, and . . . you know what, I'll just stop describing it because I'm nauseated searching for the right simile.

It got on my T-shirt. And down the front of her pajama pants.

I'd dealt with poop in a million different situations: the car, the living room, the bed, the playground, the church, the pantry.

It got in my nose. My sinuses. My throat.

I sat her down and threw up in the kitchen sink.

Mel and our two older children were at a church activity. It was a little after 7:30 p.m., and they'd stayed there later than expected, so I changed my shirt and washed my face and chest in the bathroom sink.

I used mouthwash.

Then I got Aspen in the tub.

I was standing over her, still smelling like puke, when she pooped and then gave me a satisfied smirk. It was a little brown thing, the size of a small kiwi. It drifted to the shallow end of the tub. I looked at it for a moment, not sure just what to do.

Sure, I'd dealt with poop in a million different

situations: the car, the living room, the bed, the playground, the church, the pantry. But there was something about poop in the tub that always gave me pause. Not that my children hadn't pooped in the tub before. They had. And every time I got a toddler in the tub, I knew there was a 40 percent chance that poop would happen. Is that too low? Let's say 60 percent. That sounds more accurate.

I swear, sometimes it felt like the bathtub caused my toddlers to poop . . .

I'd seen poop in the tub enough times that I should've been mentally trained for any poop-in-the-tub moment, but every time it happened, I froze, weighted with questions: *Should I get her out? Will I get poop on me? Can poop bacteria travel through water? If I don't touch it, will I still be clean? Am I going to have to touch it? Why is Aspen so happy about this? Why haven't I gotten her out yet?*

And as I thought, Aspen turned around and reached for the turd. She got half a grip on it, breaking it into smaller pieces. Then she reached for her mouth, as two-year-olds often do, and I caught her hand before she could shove it in. I tugged her out of the tub by wrapping my left arm around her waist, and I held her poopy hand with my right, her body slippery with poop water. She put up a kicking, wiggling fight, so I had to hold her close to my body. I took her to the sink and washed her hands, twice, and then mine . . . twice.

My shirt and pants were soaked now, along

with the bathroom floor. We were both freckled with baby poop. I couldn't see it, but I could feel it. I could smell it. I wanted to spray my body down with bleach.

Poop just doesn't go down a tub drain. I'm sorry, it doesn't, and I've tried a million different methods. Trust me.

As a parent, I've learned a lot about poop. In some ways, I feel like a poop expert. Like I should have a poop PhD hanging on the wall somewhere. Is that even a thing? It doesn't matter; just rest assured that I know a lot about the subject. And yet I couldn't quite figure out what to do. One thing I knew for sure: Poop just doesn't go down a tub drain. I'm sorry, it doesn't, and I've tried a million different methods. Trust me. I've used toilet paper to fish it out, which only retrieves part of the mess and, if the paper becomes soggy, feels like I might as well be using my actual hand. Once I mashed it down the drain with a McDonald's straw, which sort of worked but not really. Another time Mel had to get a spatula, fish it out, and transfer it to the toilet. (This actually worked the best. Pro tip: Throw away the spatula.)

But each previous time, Mel was home, and together we looked at the problem—the size, the shape, the consistency—and eventually came up with a strategy to handle the thing.

But this time, I was alone.

Very alone.

And dripping with poop water.

I'd never felt so overwhelmed in my whole life . . .

I set Aspen down and shut the bathroom door. I pulled the drain, and once the water was gone, toddler poop spotted the tub, the tub liner, and the baby toys in varying degrees. Some went down the drain, but most clung to anything and everything. I wanted to just light the tub on fire and start over. It seemed like it might be easier (and more sanitary) but not safe or practical.

I turned the shower on high and hot and started working what poop I could down the drain, with mixed results. I had to use my hand once to force a large chunk down, and as I touched it, felt its texture, I thought about how this was not what I had signed on for. More advanced parents always spoke in general idioms when describing parenting, like, "It takes hard work" and, "It isn't easy, but it's worth it."

But no one said anything about this.

> I wanted to just light the tub on fire and start over.

I was so focused on this regrettable task and my own misery, cursing to myself, I didn't notice that while my back was turned Aspen had gotten hold of the plunger and was now chewing on the rubbery business end. And when I spotted her, she laughed at me. A sweet toddler laugh that seemed to say, "You weren't paying attention, so I did *this* to myself. You're a failure."

All of it took fewer than thirty minutes. Thirty horrible, never-ending, seventh-circle-of-hell minutes, and I wondered how I was going to make it sixteen more years until this kid went to college.

And in that moment, I did feel like I sucked as a dad. Between the sour milk, and the throw-up, and the poop in the tub, and the gnawed-on plunger, all of it took fewer than thirty minutes. Thirty horrible, never-ending, seventh-circle-of-hell minutes, and I wondered how I was going to make it sixteen more years until this kid went to college. How was I ever going to keep her healthy and happy when so many things could go wrong in such a short amount of time?

I took the plunger away and said, "Yuck" and, "Gross" in hopes that she would understand that what she did was nasty and to never do it again. But I don't think she got that message. Instead, she just got really mad and cried and screamed, then walked over to me, naked and bowlegged, and hugged my shin, soaking my jeans in more poop water. She reached out for me to pick her up, and all I could think about was how she'd just had a plunger in her mouth, how she was wet with poop water, and how her breath probably still smelled like puke. It felt like the Swamp Thing was attacking me. Or maybe something worse? Is there anything worse than the Swamp Thing? Yes, there is: a two-year-old.

But this wasn't a movie.

It was my life.

And right then, I hated that fact.

I didn't want to hold her. I wanted to be clean, but I couldn't do that just then, so I picked her up, looked in her blue eyes, and said, "You are the nastiest person I know." She stopped crying for a moment. She didn't laugh or look offended.

She stuck her hand in my mouth.

The same hand that touched the turd.

The same hand that touched the plunger.

I pulled it out and spit, and gagged, and cried a little.

I put Aspen down again and used more mouthwash. Then I used some cleaner on the tub and the toys. I kept a close eye on her this time. Then I filled the tub again, got her in, and I lathered her with soap.

Then I did it again.

And as I washed her, she giggled and cooed and tried to tell me a story, a garbled, adorable mess of noises that sounded like words but ultimately had no meaning.

By the time I got her out and changed my

clothing once again, I stopped thinking about the nastiness we'd just gone through.

I felt confident that by the next day, I wouldn't even consider it, and there's something so depressing about that. Horrible puke and poop moments had become my life. I thought about how, if anyone else had thrown up on me, pooped in my tub, made me clean it out, and then stuck a poopy hand in my mouth, I'd have had them killed.

But with Aspen, my daughter, life, emotions, chaos—it all changed as quickly as a streetlight.

By the time Mel got home, the laundry was going, the house smelled of cleaner, and Aspen and I were playing with a toy car track in the living room. Mel said she was sorry for taking so long. Then she asked how things went, and I rolled my eyes and said, "We had some throw up and some poop. But I handled it."

"Oh," she said. "Is everything . . ."

I cut her off with my cold, dead look and said with a growl, "I handled it."

She stopped midsentence, looked me up and down, and then put her hands up and started to walk away.

"Wait," I said. "Watch Aspen. Closely. I'm going to take a long shower."

Crazy Decisions I've Made in an Attempt to Save My Carpet, Furniture, and Sanity

Two-year-olds ruin carpet, furniture, car upholstery, clothing, backyards, toys, sanity, refrigerator doors, sleep patterns . . . I could go on, but you get the idea. Two-year-olds are the Darth Vader of jacking up everything valuable. They destroy all the things, and they don't feel bad about it. Nope. And the worst part is they always cry and ask you to hold them after ruining something, and the whole time you're left looking at your sofa with a puddle of puke on it and wondering why you're not the one crying.

I've had to be vigilant. I've had to be on my

game 100 percent, ready to do anything to save the things I value until my child has enough sense to not drop their pants and pee on my Nintendo. I've made some decisions, horrible decisions that led to shameful actions, to keep my children from destroying my home.

Parenting makes you crazy.

Here are a few examples (this is not a comprehensive list).

- **Pointed a puking child's face at my chest.** When Tristan was two, he came down with this horrible puke virus that lasted a week (one of many puke fests I've endured). Until I had a child, I had no idea that a two-year-old could propel puke at a distance twice his or her own height. Living with a puking toddler is like living with that poison-spitting dinosaur in the original *Jurassic Park*. Yes, it sometimes gets in your mouth. Yes, it makes you choke. No, it won't kill you. I must have cleaned the carpet a dozen times in three days. Eventually, I got to where I could see it coming, and once Tristan made the puke face, I pointed his mouth at my chest, and let it happen. Now let me make this clear: I made a conscious decision to allow someone to puke on me because I knew changing my clothing and taking a shower was easier than shampooing the carpet. Desperate times, people. Desperate measures.

- **Thrown a potty-training child with crossed legs onto my lap.** Once I was sitting on the sofa and Norah, who was two, almost three, crossed her legs, placed her hands on her crotch, and started to cry. She was in a little summer dress and her new big-kid underwear. We were ambitious to start potty training this early, I'll admit. We were chatting with some friends at a party and they were like, "My child is two and a half and already potty trained. She can also drive a car and do calculus. You must either be horrible, neglectful parents, or your child isn't developing properly." Okay, that last part was an exaggeration, but that's what it felt like, so we tried to potty train the child too early. Anyway, when she crossed her legs, I knew I'd seen that look before, and she ended up wetting her pants and got pee all over the carpet. So I grabbed her and placed her on my lap. It got warm then. Eerily warm. As I took a shower and was doing laundry, I couldn't help but think about how much easier all that was than cleaning the carpet.

- **Banned Silly Putty.** After finding Silly Putty wedged between the cushions of my sofa, it became banned in my house. Tears, begging, I didn't care. That crap was gone.

- **Placed a two-year-old with explosive diarrhea in the kitchen sink.** Norah had some epic poops (see page 71), and one time I found her in the living room with that red-faced, "I'm pooping and it's going to be a frothy whopper" look. She was in a weighty diaper, one of those fifteen-pound numbers that two-year-olds often sport, obviously at max capacity, but no one had taken the time to handle it. There was no way it was going to hold what she was about to let go, so I lifted her up, ran into the kitchen because it was closer than the bathroom, placed her in the sink, and watched her grunt, smile, and then boil over like a chocolate fondue.

- **Allowed my children to hang from my freaking foot as I hobbled around the house.** Why did my toddlers so enjoy wrapping their arms around my shin like a sloth and ask me to drag their twenty-five-pound butts around the house? I don't know, but I've done it so many times with three children that when I look at my legs in the mirror, the right is larger than the left. I call one Biggie and the other Smalls. My hips hurt so bad that I went to the doctor. He told me that I had inflammation, and that I'd need a cortisone shot to reduce it. Although I could blame this situation on age, I'd rather blame it on my children's obsession with my dragging them around. Why did I continue to do this?

Because if I didn't they'd cry and I'm a sucker for that. It was also cute how they looked as I hobbled around and they laughed like I was an honest amusement park ride. I have no other explanation.

- **Tackled a child with dog poop on his shoes.** When Tristan was two, we lived in a small house in Provo, Utah. He and I were playing in the yard, and I watched him step in dog poop just outside the kitchen door and then go running inside. I chased down that little turd-stepper, and just before he made it from the kitchen tile to the living room carpet, I tried to reach out and grab him but ended up falling on top of him. He cried. I got dog poop on my shirt. Then I gagged. But the real crisis was avoided. I have no regrets.

- **Used my bare hands to lift a turd off the floor.** One day I was walking through my living room and noticed a turd on the floor. It must have been Norah's or Tristan's. I knew it wasn't mine, and I was about 80 percent sure it wasn't my wife's. Kidding. Kidding. I'm about 85 percent sure. We didn't have a dog or any other pet at the time. I didn't know how long it had been there, but what I do know is that I was filled with a mix of emotions. Anger that it had happened. Fear that it would stain the carpet. Anxiety about cleaning it up. All of this clouded my judgment and caused me to reach in with no protection, grab the turd, and carry it into the bathroom. Not my proudest moment.

- **Read the same story over and over until I wanted to die inside.** One hundred and seventy-two nights. We began reading *The Wheels on the Bus* in March and finally stopped reading it in September, so by my math Aspen and I read that book for 172 consecutive nights. As I write, I'm struggling to find a simile that fits how sick I was of that story, which to me means that it's comparable to nothing. It was just that painful. I was sick of the driver, sick of the horn, sick of the babies crying, and sick of the "Shh, shh, shh" that the parents go. But here's what kept me going: Each night I'd carry her to bed on my shoulders. She'd find the book and hide it behind her back, and then I'd pretend to be surprised by it. (I'd like to thank the Academy . . .) When we got to the end, and the bus parked at a birthday party, and Aspen screamed, "Happy birthday" . . . well, my heart melted.

So I've done a few crazy things to save my stuff. Am I insane? Should I be locked up? Well, I remember reading somewhere that if you aren't crazy by the time your children leave the house, then they have done something wrong. I think these early decisions in parenting that defy all logic are the foundation for that goal. Nice work, kids. Well played.

Silence Is a Scary Sound

I walked in on my two-year-old daughter Aspen silently cramming full rolls of toilet paper into the toilet, smashing them down with a toy broom, and repeatedly flushing.

There was at least an inch of water on the floor. The colorful fish-shaped bath mat was floating a bit, along with some bath toys and a bottle of shampoo. Her red dress, white leggings, blonde hair in spindly pigtails, all of her, was soaked in toilet water. I stepped into the water for a moment, barefoot, felt how cold it was, and then stepped back into the hallway.

Aspen looked at me. She didn't smile, or laugh, or speak. She just stopped what she was doing for a moment, made eye contact, and then went back to business, her face void of regret or joy or fear of reprisal, similar to the Terminator.

I cussed under my breath, then I waded into the restroom, pulled her away from the toilet, and said something that is the refrain of parenting: "I knew it was too quiet."

As a father of toddlers, I'd learned to fear quiet.

It was quiet the day Norah monkeyed open the refrigerator lock and pulled out a bottle of ketchup, squeezed it out on the floor, then rolled around in it, making condiment angels.

It was quiet the day Tristan took his Home Depot toy handsaw to my eyeglasses, busting out the lenses. It took me two weeks to get in with an optometrist because of our crappy insurance, so I couldn't drive and had to ride my bike half blind, struggling to make out bumps, and cars, and how close I was to people. I spilled out on the road a number of times and once waved and yelled excitedly to some girl I didn't know but thought was my wife, only for her to call campus police on me.

It was quiet the day Norah monkeyed open the refrigerator lock and pulled out a bottle of ketchup, squeezed it out on the floor, then rolled around in it, making condiment angels. And what did she do when I entered the room and caught her—ahem—red-handed? (See what I did there?) She slipped and fell and bumped her head, and I ended up comforting her, soaking my jeans and T-shirt in ketchup, a condiment I don't enjoy because the smell makes me gag, the whole time looking at the mess and wondering who was going to comfort *me*.

It was quiet when my son slid his toy box into the bathroom, stood on it to get to the sink, plugged it, pumped *all* the hand soap into the sink, and filled it with water, overflowing it with bubbles.

It was silent the day Aspen drank a small sample of dish soap that she fished from the garbage can. (She had diarrhea for three days.)

It was quiet when Norah snagged a full can of Pepsi from the pantry and threw it against the kitchen tile, making it rain cola and dancing as it showered down on her.

I know.

I know.

This sounds like a list of grievances, and in some ways it is. Raising toddlers is basically one big list of grievances.

But there really are two things that unite these moments: toddlers and silence.

It was silent the day Aspen drank a small sample of dish soap that she fished from the garbage can. (She had diarrhea for three days.)

Silence is scary. If my toddlers were silent, I expected them to be covered with peanut butter. I expected them to have broken my new iPhone, which happened to belong to my employer. I expected them to be examining the dog's anus.

But the really hard part, the part that makes me want to wretch as a parent, is how bad I long for silence. I want my children to be quiet like the Sahara wants water. So when it happens, it's almost difficult not to savor it. I sit and listen to it and hope that it will last forever—and rarely is my first instinct to assume that my child is up to no good, regardless of past experiences or logic, because the silence is so savory.

This is the toddler trap. They filled my world with noise and chaos so that silence was as hypnotic as a siren's song, so that the moment I heard it I'd fall into a trance while my toddler was destroying everything I loved, along with themselves, in a symphony of destruction.

Was that too dramatic?

Perhaps it was. I've just been scarred.

I've seen some things.

But the best (worst) part is this . . . because, you know, toddlers.

This is the toddler trap. They filled my world with noise and chaos so that silence was as hypnotic as a siren's song, so that the moment I heard it I'd fall into a trance while my toddler was destroying everything I loved.

Remember that story I told you about Aspen and the clogged toilet? Well, there's more. I picked up my daughter, twisted the water valve for the toilet, my face red and angry and ready for blood. And Aspen? She cried. She got all red-faced too, and I said, "Yeah. You should be crying. You're in trouble."

I put her in her room and changed her, then put down some towels in the bathroom and unclogged the toilet by fishing the toilet paper rolls out with my hands.

Aspen cried the whole time. And then, once it was all settled and she was sitting next to me on the sofa while I was telling her that what she did was naughty, she stopped crying, and she nuzzled up into my chest, and she hugged me.

She was quiet then too.

And you know what I did?

My shoulders slumped, my head went down, and I wrapped my arms around my little girl. Then I let out a breath and (get this) said, "I'm sorry I got so mad. Please don't do that again."

Then we sat on the sofa and snuggled for a bit.

I got played.

I'll admit it.

It happens time and time again with my children.

But as I sat there silently snuggling with my youngest daughter, I thought about how quiet it was, and how maybe, just maybe, silence isn't all bad.

Unsolicited Parenting Advice and How I'd Like to Respond

As a father of young children, I get a lot of unsolicited advice. Mostly from the childless and the elderly. I don't know why it's always from those two populations. I don't know why the childless are so interested in informing me about how to do a better job, as if they know anything about the job. And I don't know what happened to the elderly who give me advice as if they've forgotten what it's like to live with one of these little psychos. But it happens. And every time, I nod and say thank you graciously, as though what they have to say has actual merit. But deep inside, I want to go off on them.

Here are a few examples:

- Don't worry, son. She'll wear herself out. No, she won't! Listen, I know you're getting on in years, so I'm just going to assume that you (1) didn't have children or (2) blacked out the toddler years with alcohol. She's not going to wear herself out. She's a perpetual-motion machine that, if harnessed properly, could power the state of New York. She could run a marathon, she could swim the Atlantic, she could dig a hole to the center of the earth with her kid shovel, and I'd still be up until midnight with her kicking me in the face, or the stomach, or the crotch while she screams, "I not tired!" I know this in the core of my being, and so what I need right now is not a prediction but for you to shut your stupid face and buy your groceries.

- Why don't you just plan your time better? Then you could make it to places on time. When was the last time you tried to leave the house and someone puked on you? Have you ever tried to plan for that? Or what about shoes? How many do you put on in the morning? Two? Good for you. Do you ever take them off right before you are about to leave and hide them in the garbage can? I didn't think so. Have you ever had a passenger crap their pants the moment you got in the car? Or scream and scream and scream two blocks from the house until you turn around, run inside, and grab them some cornflakes? Have you ever asked someone to get ready to leave and they decide to get naked instead? Have you ever buckled a wolverine into a car seat? You sound like a real planner. Put all that into your schedule. Help me be on time, dickhead.

- **Listen, it's not that hard. Just sleep when they sleep.** Brilliant. For someone without kids, you're really nailing this parenting thing. Except you didn't think about the fact that I have to go to work. Or about how, when I'm home, I need a moment or two to do laundry or the dishes or to think without a booger-nosed creature attached to me. Sometimes I just need two freaking moments when I am not being drooled on to sit and be in a bubble. Yeah, sure, sleep when they sleep. Listen, I truly believe that my children wait until the most inopportune time to sleep, like in the grocery store cart, or while I'm at work, or on the freeway, so they could keep me up in the night for hours on end watching *Blue's Clues*. Do you want me to sleep on the freeway? Because I'll do it. So help me, I'll do it!

- **If you taught your child how to act at home, they'd be better behaved in public.** Shut your stupid wrinkled face. My children are sweet at home, actually. For the most part they are good little humans, but the moment I take them out into public something changes in them—kind of like what happens when a werewolf sees the moon—and suddenly they turn into fit-throwing jackwagons who roar their terrible roars and gnash their terrible teeth and roll their terrible eyes. So I take them out into public to teach them how to be respectable. Your parents did the same with you. Children learn how to act in public by going out in public, so go back to your olive martini and ranch salad and deal with it.

- **Your child wouldn't watch you pee all the time if you just locked the door.** Let me tell you how the real world works. Sometimes I can't get enough space between the child and me to lock the door. Sometimes I try to shut it, and a *PAW Patrol* light-up sneaker blocks the doorway. Sometimes I do lock the door, and then I get to listen to some near-death argument in the hallway or see little fingers creeping under the door. "Can you see them, Daddy? Can you see them?" Sometimes they sound like a SWAT team busting in on a meth house. And what about when I have to use a public restroom? What are my options there? Leave the kid to wander the store like it's 1988 and just hope they don't run into the parking lot or get kidnapped? No. You'd judge me for that, too, so I have to take them into the stall and listen to their comments on the size and smell as I repeatedly scream, "Face the wall." But hey, on the bright side, sometimes the kids barge in and offer me snacks, so that's cool.

- **If Caillou really bothers you that much, just tell the kid he can't watch it anymore. You're the parent.** Thanks for making me feel like I'm the boss of a failing company. I'm not actually in charge here. Parenting little kids is much more of a democracy with one politician on a 24-7 filibuster. I'm, like, 40 percent in charge. I'm in charge of putting his shoes on. I'm in charge of changing his diaper. I'm in charge of bath time. But when it comes to what he eats or watches, I'm not all that in charge because although he's small, he has his own opinions, wants, and needs, and he expresses them with a Donald Trump-like determination. As much as I fantasize about Caillou running with scissors, putting that whiny little baldheaded carrot pizza-eating loser on the screen gives me a few moments to myself. It keeps his attention and it stops the whining, and that, my friend, is why I let him watch that stupid show. That time is golden.

Isn't it fun to play pretend? Sure, I'd never actually say anything like this. Does that make me a pansy? Maybe . . . but probably not. Chances are, it just means that I'm a decent guy, nice enough to not make a big deal out of someone trying to help, all the while resisting the urge to punch an elderly woman in the face.

I Deserved an Award for Changing That Epic Blowout, but I Settled for a Sleeve of Oreos

The smell caught my attention. It was a funk, almost like egg salad or something else that stinks when left out of the refrigerator. It didn't smell exactly like poop, but I suppose that's what often makes toddler poop bearable. It doesn't smell quite as bad as grown-human poop, or dog poop, or any of those really nasty poops. It's not as solid either—more of a dripping brown sludge with a little grit that's the result of drinking too many juice boxes.

We were at church in Minnesota, the whole family on a bench. Mel and I were both in our late twenties, trying to make a go of it in a state where we had zero family. I was attending graduate school there. Tristan was three, almost four. He was in the cutest little dark blue pinstriped suit with a red tie that highlighted his then auburn hair. My youngest at the time, Norah, was . . . Well, I'm not sure how old she was. Was she two and one quarter? Or was she twenty-seven months? Should I have calculated this in weeks? Toddler math is the hardest math. To be honest, I'm not 100 percent sure how old she was exactly, and even if I did know, I wouldn't be able to calculate it properly, so let's just say she was two.

I thought about how we could send a man to the moon. We had internet and diet soda and white bread, and yet no one could manufacture a diaper that could contain my toddler's poop.

She wasn't saying much more than "no" and "yes." Mostly "no." I know that I didn't trust her with anything electronic, sharp, or small enough to fit down her throat. I know that she got me up in the night at times I didn't know existed before children. I mean, I'd heard of 4:00 a.m., but I don't recall actually seeing it until having children. I know that she didn't care about anything unless she could put it in her mouth, and I know that sometimes, when she pooped, it went all the way up her back like a frothy poop bath bomb, bubbling up and over the sides of her diaper. And each time it happened, I thought about how we could send a man to the moon. We had internet and diet soda and white bread, and yet no one could manufacture a diaper that could contain my toddler's poop.

She was wearing the sweetest white dress with ruffles and matching bright white shoes. She'd just started walking, which meant she was prone to falling. She walked away from me, one hand on the church pew for balance, her crooked little bowed legs pounding down with each step, her mouth all gummy and toothless, brown hair spindly and uneven. Then she fell, and a brown liquid splashed out of her diaper and soaked the back of her dress. She stood again and it leaked out from between her chubby marshmallow legs. She looked down, put some fingers in it, and just before she was about to reach in her mouth, I snagged her wrist.

"Oh, kid. What did you do?" I whispered.

The moment I touched Norah's hand, Mel and I made eye contact. She was in a long blue church dress, her brown hair in a tight braid. She was a small-framed young mother of two who wore thick-framed glasses. I was a short, stocky man in a blue dress shirt and black tie, with slacks and Chuck Taylor All Stars (my attempt to still look a little young and hip at church, despite being a father and husband). We looked at each other for a long time, both of us in a silent negotiation as to who would actually handle the poopy toddler.

This happened to us a lot. With one kid in diapers and one child potty training, it seemed like poop negotiations were a constant battle.

Score was taken: "I did it the last two times. It's your turn." Points were awarded: "The last one I did was so nasty we both needed a bath. That counts as two. Maybe even three." And negotiations were made: "If you handle it, I will have sex with you."

With one kid in diapers and one child potty training, it seemed like poop negotiations were a constant battle.

But during that moment, in church, we couldn't really negotiate. We couldn't talk it out, or keep score, or make a deal. The congregation was quiet, someone was speaking at the pulpit. Norah was starting to squirm, and pulled away from my grip. Time was short. We were only moments away from a meltdown and an epic poop mess in a church, something I have to assume would condemn us all to an eternity in hell.

We looked at each other. Our eyes didn't break for some time.

Mel looked down at my hand and raised her eyebrows.

Then she mouthed, "You touched her first."

And while that doesn't sound like something that would hold up in court, she was right. I did have my hand on the child. I did discover the mess, and chances were I'd already been contaminated.

She held out our pink and black diaper bag, two contradicting colors that we'd picked in hopes of having something neutral we both could carry and not feel awkward. I glared at her. She glared back then gave me a half-grin.

She knew she'd won.

> With Norah, each and every time it was a ruined-the-outfit, going-to-need-to-light-the-car-seat-on-fire-and-start-over, found-some-in-her-socks sort of engagement.

I took the bag, angrily slung it over my shoulder, and carried Norah out of the chapel, my hands in her armpits, arms outstretched, as though she were a leaky bucket full of steaming toxic waste.

At the time, I wondered if it were just my child. Perhaps she had an overactive colon . . . or something. Tristan had the occasional blowout. All kids do. But with Norah, each and every time it was a ruined-the-outfit, going-to-need-to-light-the-car-seat-on-fire-and-start-over, found-some-in-her-socks sort of engagement.

There's something about a blowout that makes me squirm. I think it makes all parents squirm. I'd handled so much poop, and the thought was that I might get used to it. That poop would become as ubiquitous as body sweat, and it did, to a point. Eventually I stopped gagging so much, but the reality was that it never stopped bothering me. And I surely never got to the point that I enjoyed it.

And most importantly, I never stopped feeling picked on when I had to handle a really nasty one.

It was a crappy situation all around (pardon the pun). And as I hauled the child into the restroom, I felt slighted. I felt like I should be above handling this sort of mess, or something. I felt like someone needed to be blamed, and I couldn't blame my daughter for this misfortune because she was a child. I wanted to blame my wife, but I didn't have the heart. So I looked up and gave God the side-eye.

You did this to me, I thought.

Once I made it to the restroom, placed Norah on the changing table, and saw the brown streak up her back—all the way to her neck and down her legs, some of it in her shiny white dress shoes—it was easy to see that I was going to be in it up to my elbows. I cursed in a church. (I know, I know.) I tried to take off her soiled dress and onesie and got it on her face. She wiggled and cried and fought, and by the time I got her undressed and ready to be wiped down, I realized that we had only two wipes when this was obviously a full-box-of-wipes kind of job.

And right then, as I dug deeper into the bag searching for more wipes with one hand while holding Norah on the table with the other, growing angrier and angrier, wondering whose fault it was that the diaper bag wasn't fully replenished—Mel's or mine—Norah sprawled out all naked and slimy as a seal after an oil spill, the lights went out.

There were no windows.

It was as black as the deep, dark cave I wanted to run away to and live in.

Norah started to cry.

I wanted to cry.

At the time, I owned a flip phone, so I opened it up and did what I could with the light from the screen. I stumbled around and found the toilet paper. I used part of my shirt out of desperation.

I stood in the dark for a moment, Norah crying on the changing table, and let out a deep breath.

I once got lost in the woods on my mountain bike outside Jackson Hole, Wyoming. Like really, really, lost. The sun was almost down, and I heard some howling in the distance as the moon peeked over the mountains. Naturally, I found my way out. But there was a moment when I felt completely hopeless. For the first time in my life, death was a stone's throw away. But I didn't feel nearly as hopeless in the woods as I felt trying to change my daughter's epic blowout in the dark.

I looked up again and asked for a miracle, and suddenly the lights came on as someone entered the restroom. It was then that I realized the power hadn't gone out, but rather the changing table was in the far corner of the restroom, in the handicapped stall, and the light sensor couldn't see my motion.

As the man entered the restroom, all of this became apparent, and suddenly I didn't know if I should feel grateful or enraged. But none of those emotions lasted long as I looked down to see the full extent of the damage.

My shirt, tie, and slacks were soiled. The white tips of my All Stars were spackled with it, and there were small poop handprints on the wall and along the changing table, making it almost look like there was an epic struggle, which there was, but I really didn't want there to be evidence. Norah was still naked, only half clean and still slimy, her adorable white dress in a nasty heap on the restroom tile. When I think back on this moment, I realize that if a miracle happened that day, it was that a twenty-five-pound child could produce that much poop.

I didn't know the man who entered the restroom. He was the father of another student from my college, in town to visit his son. The restroom stall was open. He poked his head inside, his hand covering his nose from the smell, and said, "You okay? What happened?"

He had gray hair with a matching beard and suit. He wore a black tie and shoes. His eyes were open wide.

I turned, one hand on Norah, and lifted the other, and said, "Please don't look at me."

There was a deep sorrow in my voice, a shame that cannot be translated into words that I will forever feel each time I relive this moment at 3:00 a.m.

The man seemed to want to say more. Perhaps he wanted to ask if I needed help, but instead, he just looked me up and down, surveying the situation one more time, and stepped out, leaving me alone with my daughter, the mess, and what was left of my dignity.

> There was a deep sorrow in my voice, a shame that cannot be translated into words that I will forever feel each time I relive this moment at 3:00 a.m.

I cleaned the wall and changing table as best I could. I collected our belongings and I collected my thoughts. I wondered if there was a lesson to be learned here. I wondered if God was trying to teach me something. Be more prepared, maybe? Expect the unexpected? Life is shit? No, that's too obvious.

As I left the church on a parental walk of shame: shoulders rigid, face tight, looking behind me for witnesses, Norah in nothing but a new diaper, stink lines coming off both of us, I realized that sometimes life doesn't teach you lessons.

Sometimes life just sucks.

Sometimes it's okay to question your life choices in a church parking lot.

Sometimes it's okay to eat a sleeve of Oreos.

Things I Will Bill My Kids for Once They Are Adults (Plus Inflation)

———————————————————

There are some things you just can't quantify. Love, for example. Dedication, passion, sanity. I don't know their value. I studied English. But what I can say is this: My children owe me. Big time. Each year I go further into financial and emotional debt with these adorable little goblins. And someday I expect payment in full. Not in kisses, or hugs, or visits from grandkids, although those will always be appreciated.

Someday I'm going to expect cash money from my children, plus inflation.

I've stayed awake many nights keeping a running mental tab, and now I'm pleased to present the first draft of things I will bill my children for once they are adults.

- **Three sofas.** Yes, they were used sofas. Yes, I was smart enough to buy them at yard sales until my children were old enough to manage their pee and poop and hold a cup without a lid. But still . . . *three* sofas? All of them stained, or ripped, or stained and ripped. All of them had a funk I couldn't get out. And trust me, I tried it all (shampoo, carpet cleaner, professional steam cleaners, magic). Just thinking about it turns on my dad rage.

- **Therapy.** Aspen once shoved a popcorn kernel in her nose and we had to have a doctor get it out. Sometimes I lie awake at night in a cold sweat, my hand clutching my chest, over this. My therapist and I still talk about it.

- **Six years of carpet cleaning.** Six *years*!

- **Hours of mindless videos on YouTube Kids.** I should be compensated for this because there are some things I just can't wipe from my memory. Like "The Finger Family Song," magic egg videos, and that stupid song about that Johnny kid stealing sugar. Listen to me: The road to hell was paved by Ryan Toys Review.

- **Summer water bill for six years of unnecessary sprinkler usage.** The kids asked to play in the sprinkler—and asked, and asked, and asked, until I either turned it on or plunged my head into a bucket of water to drown it all out.

- **Grass seed and fertilizer.** This charge is for six years of replanting the large dead-grass circle because of the backyard kids' pool.

- **Vet bills.** Sometimes being a dad meant I got to hold Queen Elsa's ice wand high over my head so she'd stop trying to stick it in the dog's butt. And sometimes being a dad meant taking the dog to the vet to make sure his butthole was okay.

- **Wasted food.** How many times was I asked for food, then I made the food, then the food was refused, so it ended up being (a) thrown away; (b) eaten by me; (c) fed to the dog, which made him throw up, stain the carpet, and result in a trip to the vet (the cost of which can be added to several line items above)? The answer is somewhere between a million and the weight of the sun.

- **Gym membership for years.** This membership was needed to work off all those extra Pop-Tarts crusts, mashed potatoes, and Lucky Charms (minus the marshmallows) that I ate because they refused to, and I didn't have any self-control.

- **After-hours pay.** For obvious reasons.

- **One million gallons of gas.** Used while driving in circles to get my toddlers to sleep.

- **One million gallons of caffeine.** Toddlers don't sleep.

- **Doctor bills.** Listen, I'm not going to charge my kids for being born. I take responsibility for that. But how many times did they refuse to wash their hands? How many times did they shove germ-infested toys in their mouth? How many times did they cough in my face or shove their booger hands in my mouth? I'll tell you: Infinity. And how many times did they get me sick? Also infinity.

- **Toxic waste disposal.** Professionals get paid good money to handle this sort of stuff. And I handled a lot of it.

- **Toys.** Just the ones we purchased that they played with once or until they decided the box was cooler than the toy.

- **Vacuum replacement and repair bills.** I don't care if it's commercial grade, a vacuum is not built to suck up LEGOs, Barbies, or Shopkins that are placed all over the house like landmines.

- **DVD player.** Sure, these things aren't worth much *now*—but back in the day, Tristan crammed ours full of peanut butter, and I'm still not over it.

- **Missing socks.** One hundred million pairs!

- **Van detailing.** It was either that or drive it off a cliff.

I get it. You are like, *Where's the cost on this, Clint? Where are the numbers? What about the cost of inflation? How bad are you going to stick it to those toddlers? It must be well over a million dollars!*

I thought about adding some estimates, but as I wrote this list, something came to me. I realized parenthood is universal. They will get what's coming to them when they have children of their own.

Locking Doors
Is Hilarious Until
the Fire Department
Arrives

Norah was laughing in her bedroom, and when I tried to open the door, it was locked.

I pushed on the door.

She tugged at the knob.

I could see her shadow along the carpet.

She was two, close to three, and we were renting a small two-level town house in Minnesota. I was twenty-eight and in graduate school. It was midmorning on a weekday in the summer, so I was home.

This wasn't the first time she'd locked herself in a room. She'd recently figured out how to lock a door, so she did it *all* the time. She thought it was hilarious to lock the upstairs bathroom door with no one inside and then laugh, her hand on her little stomach, when I found out. She locked herself in our bedroom and then laughed and laughed as I popped it open with a screwdriver. She was really good at locking doors. She had that down, but she hadn't figured out how to *unlock* them.

I'd gotten pretty good at picking locks in the house with a slender, three-inch long, green-handled screwdriver from our junk drawer.

Not that I'm a handy person or anything. If you could see my hands right now, as they type, you'd see soft, tender skin. No calluses, or cuts, or cracks, or scars from actual manual labor.

They smell like lavender because I use lotion.

I once fixed our bathtub sink and swore so much that Mel had to take the kids out of the house.

Remember on *Seinfeld* when George Costanza became a hand model? I'm kind of like that . . .

I mean, don't get me wrong, I've worked with my hands. I once changed my own oil. That was a big deal. And I have swung an ax a time or two. In a former life, in my early twenties, I tried to be a power lineman—but that ended after I almost died a handful of times.

I once fixed our bathtub sink and swore so much that Mel had to take the kids out of the house. I did fix it, for a week or so. Then it broke again, and we ended up calling a plumber because it was leaking behind the wall, ruining our crawl space with shame water, each *drip*, *drip*, *drip* a reminder that I'm not at all handy, which kind of, sort of, translated to a chip in my masculinity.

I did get pretty good at popping a lock during this time, and that felt significant. However, I know there's at least one handy person reading this, rolling their eyes like I did when my now eleven-year-old son learned how to make pancakes and then acted like he could live on his own. But just bear with me, please. Let me have my moment of satisfaction, because, like so many of my stories do, it all comes crashing down, so your real opportunity to feel superior is closer to the end of this chapter.

I told Norah not to worry. "I got this, kiddo."

I left for a moment, and as I did, Norah went from laughing to crying and tugging and twisting the doorknob.

I came back with the screwdriver. I hunched down to pop the lock, and realized that this lock was different than the others in our town house. A few days earlier, this had been Tristan's room. But the kids wanted to swap rooms, so we did, and for the first time I realized that on this bedroom door was an exterior lock with a keyhole that fit a key I didn't have.

By this point, Norah was on her hands and knees, reaching her little fingers under the door, crying. I'm not sure how long she'd been locked in the room, but there is something about a moment like this that makes time stretch out.

Minutes felt like hours.

I started to panic.

I didn't own a ladder, so I couldn't go in through Norah's second-story window. Not that I'd have any idea how to open a locked window once I got up there. I thought about kicking in the door, but her hands were stretched out under it, and when I asked her to back up, she just stuck her fingers farther under the door and cried harder. I told her how to unlock the door, but she was a two-year-old, so it felt like I was trying to tell a mongoose how to ring a doorbell.

Mel was in the hallway now, trying to help. I was on my hands and knees, holding Norah's fingers to give her comfort, looking at the lock, stumped.

Mel stood over me, shoeless, in blue jeans and a green T-shirt. I showed her the lock and how I didn't know what to do. She looked a little scared, but not nearly as scared as I felt.

"Can we use a credit card or something?" she suggested. "I've seen that in movies."

"I don't know, babe. That sounds like a long shot," I said. "Where would we even stick it?"

"I don't know," she said. "I think right there." She pointed between the door and the frame, to the right of the doorknob.

"Do we jab at it, or is it an up-and-down motion?

Is there a twist we should be doing? Ugh . . . this is all so complicated."

Mel shrugged.

At the time I was a graduate student studying English, and Mel was working on a degree in horticulture. When I think about this conversation, I feel like we were the protagonists in a joke that begins with, "An English major and a horticulturalist tried to pick a lock . . ."

I suppose the main problem was that both of us were so used to discussing the theory of something that the thought of taking action before discussing our motives, goals, and outcomes seemed foreign.

We were about as comfortable in this situation as a locksmith might be in a graduate-level literary theory class.

Our discussion on how best to pick a lock with a credit card ended when Norah's cries changed from ones of panic to deep, helpless, animal-like moans that made me wonder if she'd locked herself in her room in order to transform into a wolflike creature.

I went through my wallet and found an old debit card and wedged it between the door and the frame. It didn't work. I just ended up ripping the card. But it gave me an idea, so I started trying other things. I tried a spatula, a butter knife, a screwdriver, more cards, and so on. I chipped up the doorframe. I said a number of prayers in my head. I hoped for inspiration. I asked for divine intervention.

Nothing.

Nothing worked, and by the end, I'd worn the skin off my index finger and was now bleeding.

Somewhere in all of this, Tristan joined us. He was four, close to five, and he looked a little too excited. Suspiciously excited, his hands clapping occasionally, toes tapping.

"Is Norah in there forever?" he asked, one hand cupped into the other.

This was the first time I realized my four-year-old son was a narcissist and wanted the worst for Norah.

He was in jean overalls and a black T-shirt with the bones of a *T. rex* on it. He was smiling a big, happy smile. It was the same smile he gave when he won an argument with his sister, or when he got to pick where we went for a Saturday activity. He was, I have no doubt, thrilled by the idea of his little sister being locked in a room for the rest of her life.

"No, no," I said. "I'll get her out."

Tristan frowned a little. Then he went back into the living room and played with his toy trucks.

This was the first time I realized my four-year-old son was a narcissist and wanted the worst for Norah.

I wanted to pull him aside and lecture him about how his sister was part of this family, too, and that locking her in a room was rude and mean and ultimately a federal crime, but I didn't have the time.

I must admit, however, that as I spoke with my son, I was struck with this horrible notion: Perhaps she *was* going to be in there forever. Perhaps we'd have to feed her by shoving food under the door.

I was freaking out.
I'm sure you've noticed.

Perhaps this would all result in a *Dateline* investigation, where Mel and I would sit in a white room, a spotlight on us, and the host would ask difficult questions like, "Why did you allow your daughter to be locked in a room until she was twenty?" and I'd stutter and try to blame it on food additives and a political party.

I was freaking out.

I'm sure you've noticed.

During this time Mel called a locksmith. We didn't have any family in the area, and this was a few years before YouTube how-to videos really started to take off, so I didn't even think to search for a tutorial. It was the middle of a workday, and everyone we knew either had jobs or were college students about as handy as I was. I did call a few people that I thought might be able to assist, but no one answered, and in some ways I was grateful they didn't. Just the thought of trying to explain the situation felt like I was admitting guilt: "Hey, dude. I'm a crappy, neglectful parent with no mechanical ability. Can you come help me get my daughter out of her room? She's locked in there and I'm pretty sure she's turning into a werewolf."

In many ways, it felt like the best thing to do was to call a simple anonymous service worker who could fix the problem, collect a fee (and perhaps a tip to keep quiet), and then leave. We'd never see him or her again. Thinking back now, this seems like a very ridiculous and selfish assumption. Norah was terrified and locked in her room while I was worried about my reputation.

We lived in a small city in southern Minnesota, so there were only three locksmiths listed. Mel called all of them but found only one who was available to come help. The rest had appointments, and although we explained the situation to them, and they could obviously hear Norah screaming in the background, they weren't willing to modify their schedules.

When my kids were born, the hospital sent me home with a few things on caring for my child, but most of them were about the importance of not shaking a baby—the rest were bills and instructions on how to pay them. The doctor should've given me something with a section titled "What to Do When a Toddler Locks Herself in Her Room." The chapter would be between "How to Keep a Child from Throwing a Fit in a Store," and "How to Not Be Offended When Your Baby Boy Pees in Your Face." Every day as a parent, I felt like I was faced with a new challenge, and every time I felt like I should've had more training from the government, God, or someone before I was allowed to take the child home.

Norah had been locked in her room for close to an hour when I ran out of objects to cram between the door and the frame. Almost everything I tried either got chewed up or bent. Mel checked her phone and noticed that the locksmith had called. Apparently he knocked on the door, but we couldn't hear him because of Norah's screaming. When Mel called him back, he said that since we didn't answer, he went to another job and couldn't come back for two more hours.

Every day as a parent, I felt like I was faced with a new challenge, and every time I felt like I should've had more training from the government, God, or someone before I was allowed to take the child home.

I've never seen Mel so angry in my life. (This included *all* the stupid things I'd done up to that point, and trust me, there were some whoppers.) Her face was red and her left hand was in a tight fist. She didn't scream at the guy, but I wish she had. Instead, she hung up the phone while he was midsentence. Then she threw it across the room. "What a jerk," she said. "What a stupid jerk!"

Then she sat on the sofa, head in her hands, and cried.

Norah stopped screaming around this time, and I wondered if she'd moved from behind the door. I got down on the floor and looked through the crack between the door and the carpet. I closed one eye, and I could see Norah, lying on the floor doing the same thing. She was trying to see if anyone was still out there, and when she saw my eye, she started screaming again.

It was then that I called the police.

The operator had a soft voice that somehow still carried authority. I told her about the situation and assumed she was going to send a SWAT team, along with a few social workers, to teach me how to be a responsible parent. Instead she said, "I'm sorry, sir, but that really isn't an emergency."

I recall feeling a little offended, but mostly I just felt helpless. My two-year-old was locked in a room, and had been for some time, and that wasn't an emergency?

"Listen," I said. "I am out of ideas here. I've been trying to get in there for an hour. We've called several locksmiths, and none of them can be here in fewer than two hours. I'm freaking out. My wife's freaking out. And if you listen, you can tell that my daughter is freaking out. Please come and help me. I don't know what else to do."

I don't know if it was the helplessness in my voice or the crying in the background, but the operator paused for a moment. I could hear her speaking to someone else. Then she said, "What's your address?"

Ten minutes later, a fire truck and two police cars arrived at my house. They had their lights on but not their sirens. Three police officers and two firefighters, in full uniforms, came up my stairs with a box of tools. I thought Tristan's head was going to explode. This was, hands down, the coolest thing he'd ever seen. And me? I was hot with embarrassment. I was grateful for the help, but at the same time I couldn't believe that it would take this many people to help me get through a locked bedroom door to my daughter. It seemed like too much. It felt like they'd sent out something over the wire that read, "Code 20: Underqualified father needs help opening bedroom door."

The officers and firefighters were gracious.

A slender police officer with brown hair and a mustache pulled me to the side and said, "This happens to the best of us." I assumed he was the guy with some sort of crisis training.

The firefighters stood outside the bedroom door and discussed kicking it in but realized Norah was too close to it. They went through a few of the ideas I had, but eventually they wedged a slender tool between the door and the frame, hit it with a mallet, and the door popped open.

Norah's brown hair, soft face, small hands, pink neck—everything—was dripping with tears and boogers, and her diaper was leaking out the sides of her pink-footed PJs. She looked up at the group of men standing at her door with silent terror.

Then she saw Mel just behind them and ran to her mother. As she and Mel hugged, the men in the room let out a tender, "Aww."

The officers and firefighters left about as quickly as they came, and suddenly it was quiet in the house.

I took the lock off Norah's door so this wouldn't happen again.

That night, once the kids were in bed and Mel and I were sitting on the sofa, unwinding in front of the TV, she said, "I was really proud of the way you told the 911 operator that we were out of options."

"What are you saying, exactly?" I asked.

"It was just . . ." She shrugged. "Very manly, the way you told her what we needed. You didn't give up. It was kind of sexy."

"Really?" I said, a few octaves higher than normal. Then I said it again in a deeper, more masculine voice. "*Really?*"

She nodded.

I smiled and laughed a little.

Then I put my hand up and she gave me a high five.

You Know What's Worse than Waiting in the Van with a Toddler? Shopping with a Toddler . . .

Aspen was unbuckled and standing on my lap in the front seat, turning the steering wheel, playing with any knob she could find, wiping drool and boogers and who knows what on the dashboard (and my shirt, and my jeans), and smelling like applesauce and fruit snacks. She'd taken her shoes off because that's what two-year-olds do. She was in pink leggings and a white onesie, a five-inch-round dark drool spot on the front of her shirt because she was teething, a pink Binky attached to her shoulder with a green tether.

She was giggling.

I wasn't.

I was grumbling because it felt like being trapped in a hot cage with a wild honey badger on a pot of coffee, her mouth spackled with Goldfish crackers.

Mel was picking up a few things at Costco.

Our two older kids were at friends' houses. We lived in a small, rural Oregon town, and the playdate for our older two was forty-five minutes away in a larger town with an abundance of places to shop—so after we dropped off Tristan and Norah, Mel suggested we take the opportunity to do some shopping, which basically translated to me driving from one store to another and sitting in the parking lot with a hyper and overly curious blonde two-year-old that no one ever wanted to watch because she was *that* child.

Each time, I felt walked on, metaphorically and physically: I literally had to guard my crotch to keep Aspen from stomping on it.

This happened to me a lot living in a small town. We'd go to some far-away town with an abundance of stores for one reason or another: a doctor's appointment, the zoo, the science museum. And it just made sense to stop at a few stores while we were in town.

I don't want to speak for Mel, but I'm pretty sure she loved it when I watched the kids in the van.

I didn't.

Each time, I felt walked on, metaphorically and physically: I literally had to guard my crotch to keep Aspen from stomping on it.

I'd probably spent close to half my life as a father in the van-the kids complaining, screaming, fighting, or climbing around and making a mess-feeling like I was trapped in Lord of the Flies while my wife "grabbed a few things."

During our first stop at a grocery store, I tried to keep her strapped in the car seat, and I will admit, that worked for a little while. She just looked out the window at people passing by while I played on my phone. But it was short-lived, and eventually she started to scream and squirm and act like she was actually strapped in an iron maiden. I drove circles around the parking lot to try to get her to go to sleep. I gave her books, and toys, and snacks, and even my phone—and all of it held her attention for only two, maybe three, minutes. We went to a shoe store then a craft store, and by the time we made it to Costco, we were on our fourth stop, and I'd been trapped in our minivan for close to two hours with the little psycho, completely out of ideas on how to entertain her. So I just let her climb around the van, banging on the windows, as I looked at the ceiling and searched for my power animal.

I'd probably spent close to half my life as a father in the van—the kids complaining, screaming, fighting, or climbing around and making a mess— feeling like I was trapped in *Lord of the Flies* while my wife "grabbed a few things" (which always turned out to be a bunch of things). And by the time she made it back, the van was on fire and the kids had killed a wild boar.

With each stop that day, Mel smiled at me, gave me a quick kiss, then exited the car quickly, as though she'd just dropped a ball and chain from her ankle and was now running off to live a free life.

With each return, I complained. I asked if this was the last stop. How many more stops did we have? Could she be a little faster? Did she realize how bad this sucked for me? Did she even care about any of that? Why was she doing this to me? Did she hate me? Did she have any idea how many times I'd been kicked in the crotch so far? And each time I complained, Mel gave me a short pep talk on how much she appreciated me, how wonderful a husband I was, and how she understood my pain and acknowledged it. "I love you," she said. By the time we made it to the next store, I was feeling better about the whole situation because of her validation, and by the time she made it back to the van with her items, I was ready to crack once again and she worked to rebuild me.

It was a pretty turbulent cycle, and I must admit that each subsequent rebuild didn't work nearly as well as the previous—I kept going further and further into a frustrated emotional hole.

Sometimes it felt like "I will wait in the van with the kids while they climb on the upholstery, mess with the windows, and take off their clothing and I desperately try not to abandon them on the nearest church's steps while you shop" was listed on our wedding vows.

Aspen wiggled on my lap. She honked the horn, nearly giving some elderly lady walking past a heart attack. Then she got mad because I wouldn't let her honk the horn anymore. We wrestled. She overpowered me twice, honking the horn again. I was sweating. It was a rainy forty degrees outside and I was sweating.

Aspen pooped, and by the time Mel made it back to the van with a cart full of huge Costco boxed items, I was changing Aspen on the front seat of the van, angry and feeling picked on.

I was done.

Mel opened the back of the van and started loading boxes. She seemed cool, comfortable, collected, her face as calm as a day spa.

I looked at her over the van seats, eyes a little crazy, and said, "You know what, I'm not doing this anymore. I'm not waiting in the van one more time with this . . ." I thought of a few swears, a few childish names, a few things no father should ever say about their own child, and eventually landed on, "Kid!"

Mel was in blue jeans, sneakers, and a purple raincoat with the hood up. She stopped loading the car, her shoulders sagging and hands limp at her sides, and said, "Seriously? How bad can it actually be in here with her? There's no way it's worse than bringing her into a store."

> Shopping with Aspen at age two was basically a repetitive hell of asking and wanting and begging and fit-throwing with a layer of drool. She was a huge factor in my decision to get a vasectomy.

I viewed her tucked chin, flat lips, and tight shoulders as being uncompromising. But I was pretty frustrated, and I don't know if I was thinking 100 percent clearly. Because now, as I write, it seems like Mel was closer to a mix of panic and exhaustion. The thought of taking the child into the store one more time this week was probably more than she had strength for.

Aspen was a terror. She snagged things from shelves. She broke things. Shopping with Aspen at age two was basically a repetitive hell of asking and wanting and begging and fit-throwing with a layer of drool. She was a huge factor in my decision to get a vasectomy.

Don't get me wrong, I love the kid. But holy moly, she was a handful.

But I didn't think about any of that. I'd been stuck in that van so long I thought nothing—not sitting in boiling water, not swimming in a lake full of piranhas, not the van backing over my head—could be worse than spending one more minute with my two-year-old daughter in a parking lot.

"It's way worse," I said. "I'm not doing it anymore."

I presented her with options. I told her I could go into the store, and she could wait in the van. I could wait in the van alone while she took Aspen in. Eventually, we settled on all of us going into the store.

Our next stop was Target.

We loaded Aspen into the cart, neither of us speaking. We went into the store, and then I did something I'm not proud of: I felt like I deserved a break. I told Mel I needed to use the restroom, which I did—then I wandered the store for probably fifteen or twenty minutes as Mel shopped, alone, with our toddler.

I just wanted a little time not being touched, or clawed at, or drooled on. I looked at the novelty T-shirts. I picked one out. I checked out the dollar section. Eventually I caught back up with Mel to find Aspen on the floor, flailing dramatically, arms and legs spread, stomach down, screaming because she wanted a bottle of cough syrup that she thought was juice.

Mel picked up Aspen and held her. Aspen screamed, and kicked, and beat her forearms against Mel's back. She was screaming loud enough that Mel scrunched her face and tilted her head because it was hurting her ear.

I looked around.

People were watching.

It was one of those four-alarm meltdowns. The ones strangers love to gawk at.

Everything about Mel showed of deep weariness. It seemed to be beyond anything I'd ever felt as a father. It was far beyond what I felt being in the van with a two-year-old. Mel looked like she'd been wandering in the wilderness for years with no clear hope on the horizon.

I thought about the last time I'd gone to the store alone with Aspen. It'd been quite a while ago. Probably a month or more. Then I thought about how I went to the gas station, grocery store, bank, doctor, dentist, department store, and a million other places without kids all the time. Going anywhere without children was my norm.

Mel's norm was the opposite.

Mel was a part-time teacher and a full-time mom. More often than not, she had all three children with her, one in the cart asking to get out and two at her side, dragging their feet and begging for candy and toys and any other thing that caught their attention. In comparison, sitting in the van with my kids for an hour or more on a Saturday seemed a million times easier.

Mel grabbed her purse from the cart. I could tell

she was about to abandon the shopping trip and take Aspen to the van.

I approached Mel.

I took Aspen, and she looked at me with a start, blue eyes open wide, expecting it to have been Mel again, only to realize it was Dad. The shock broke her fit. I bounced her on my hip.

Mel looked at me, eyes narrow, lips in a flat line, her face saying, "Look at this. Just look at it!"

In a cold, deep, restless, I-hope-you-die-in-your-sleep voice, she said, "Where have you been?"

I didn't explain myself. I didn't tell her that I'd had a change of heart, or that I was sorry, or that I'd be happy to sit in the van when needed.

I just got Aspen calm.

She had one more fit before we left, but not nearly as bad as the first.

In a cold, deep, restless,
I-hope-you-die-in-your-sleep voice, she said,
"Where have you been?"

Once we were all loaded in the van, I sat in the driver's seat, smiled at my wife, and asked where we were going next.

"I don't . . . know," she said. She gave me a suspicious glance from the passenger seat. "Aren't you going to ask if we are done yet?"

I let out a breath. I gave it some thought. And then I said, "After watching Aspen throw that fit, I realized waiting in the van with her isn't nearly as bad as shopping with her."

She gave me another side-eye.

"I'll power through . . . somehow," I said with a wink.

She thought for a moment—and then she asked to go to Old Navy.

Crazy Things Said While Up in the Night with a Toddler

Getting up in the night with a toddler sucks. It sucks really bad. It's stressful and maddening. Mel and I have said some angry, spiteful, and sometimes irrational things to each other and the children when sleep deprived. Both of us realize that what we are saying is drafted somewhere between dream and reality and not representative of our regular feelings toward each other or the kids. So early on, we decided not to hold grudges because of what was said in the night. Following are a few examples. Names have been removed to protect the innocent.

- "It's your turn. I was just up for an hour listening to her cry and your stupid snoring. You sound like you're dying. I think I'm dying."

- "I don't know where Bun-Bun is and I don't care. Go to sleep. I've been up for more than an hour with you. If you don't go to sleep, I'm going to find Bun-Bun and light him on fire."

- "I left a wet Pull-Ups in her bed. Or maybe I put it in the laundry. I don't know—I'm too tired. Will you figure it out?"

- *"You have had enough water!"*

- "He won't sleep because his bum burns. It's probably because of his diaper rash. Can we just pack his butt with ice or something?"

- "Thanks for getting up with her. It makes me want you. I'm too tired, but I wanted you to know about it."

- "Stop asking me for string cheese. It's 4:00 a.m.! I'm going to eat all the string cheese! And you will have none, and I will have a tummy ache. I hate string cheese!"

- "She pooped in her bed and you have gas! It smells horrible in here. I swear, if you fart one more time, I'm going to kill you."

- "He wet the bed, but it's cool. I took off his pants and put down some towels."

- "I love you, but if you don't go to sleep, I might die. Is that what you want? For me to die because I feel like I'm dying. Do you even care?"

- "If you slam one more door, I'm going to take all the doors off the hinges and shove them up your butt."

- "Turn off the bathroom light! You don't need light to pee! I pee in the dark all the time."

- "Listen, I know that your tummy hurts. I get that. But you need to puke in the bowl, okay? It's not that hard. Just stick your stupid face in there and let out your stupid puke into the stupid bowl!"

- "Why am I crying? Because every time I fall asleep, she cries, or you kick me, or he asks me to put his blanket back on. Every time! I just want to drive into the ocean."

- "Sometimes, when I'm up with the kids like this, it feels like I'm in a dark hole."

- "I think you're sleeping through this because you *hate me!*"

- "If you go to sleep right now, I'll give you a whole box of cookies for breakfast."

- "If you just let me sleep for thirty more minutes, I won't have to kill anyone. Got it? *Got it?*"

- "So this is why some animals eat their young."

- "I don't know where your Binky is, but when I find it, I swear on everything holy that I'm going to tape it to your face!"

- "We had a deal. I had sex with you so you'd get up in the morning, okay? *Okay?* Stop trying to get out of the deal!"

- "I've been up for two hours watching YouTube videos of kids opening plastic eggs and now I just want to die."

- "It's four a.m. I can't peek or boo right now. Peek and boo all gone. Nod if you understand."

- "We ran out of milk! That's why I'm crying!"

- "You only get the *PAW Patrol* underwear if you stop crapping yourself in the night! It's not that difficult! This is why you don't have any friends."

- "I'm positive she hates us. That's why she's not sleeping. Only hate could do this."

- "I went to bed with puke on my shirt. Is this what rock bottom looks like?"

- "Stop touching me. I've been up with you for an hour. We're not friends."

- "I'm wiping your butt. Why are you crying? *I* should be crying."

- "Do you see anyone else laughing? Huh? Do you? It's like you're on drugs. I want some drugs . . ."

- "Just tell me what you want! Not everything is a secret!"

- "Stop being cute. No one is cute right now. I hate everything that's cute."

- "Why are you smiling? Now I'm smiling. I hate that we are smiling."

Now listen, this was a confession, right? We can confess here. This is a safe place. Would I ever say any of these things in the light of day? No. I can say this confidently. But when I've been up for hours and hours with a toddler, I'm just not myself. So I say what comes out, and I apologize in the morning if needed. And most importantly, I stay off Twitter. Anything I'd write on social while up in the night with a toddler could probably get me arrested.

Toddler-Induced Temporary Insanity

Mel greeted me at the door makeup-less, brown hair in a messy ponytail, faded blue pajama pants falling down on her left hip, underwear showing, our toddler in her outstretched arms.

"Take this," she said.

Aspen was crying and boogery and wearing nothing but a ready-to-leak-out-the-sides Costco brand diaper.

Mel wasn't using her angry voice or her playful voice but rather a voice of irritated exhaustion that lands between madness and rage. It was a low growl, deep in her throat, that I'd never heard until we had a toddler. Her bloodshot eyes, her unbrushed teeth, our living room full of toys and clothing and crumbs: Everything about this scene told me that deep inside she was fighting the urge to blow up the house and run off into the street, something similar to when the Joker destroyed that hospital in *The Dark Knight*.

Was she crazy? Well, I'm not qualified to answer that question, but my best guess would be that she was suffering from toddler-induced temporary insanity. (Please tell me this is a real thing.) And I knew where she was. I'd spent time in the asylum.

Being with Aspen alone all day felt like I was on a commercial airplane plummeting to earth. Sometimes I didn't know if I was forward or backward, and the sun, the horizon, the land, all of it blurred together into a sticky mess of milk and fruit snacks. There were four stages, really: (1) At the beginning of the descent I was optimistic that somehow we'd pull out of it; (2) I became fearful because I didn't want to die, but death seemed very plausible; (3) I accepted my fate, while angry at my decision to board the plane; (4) a fiery death.

This can happen. Dads can have a stressful day at work that is equally comparable to a stressful day with a toddler.

Mel was at stage three, no doubt about it.

But here's the kicker: I'd had a pretty stressful day myself. Calm down, stay-at-home moms. Don't throw the book across the room. This can happen. Dads can have a stressful day at work that is equally comparable to a stressful day with a toddler.

Let me explain.

At the time, I worked at a university as an academic counselor in a program that served under-represented students. A friend once described my job as the "social work of higher education," and I think that was a good assessment. One of my students had been arrested the night before. He was facing felony charges, so I'd spent a good amount of time chatting with university legal services, trying to help make sense of the situation. Trying to make sure that he got a fair shake as a low-income man of color. I didn't have the kind of frazzled weariness Mel had from a long day with a toddler, but more of an emotional and mental weariness. I was anxious right down to my fingers. Taking that toddler felt a lot like boarding a plane that I knew was going to crash.

I didn't have the strength.

"Hold on a moment," I said. "Let me put down my bag. I've had a long day." I was going to say more, but before I could, Mel cut me off. Mel set Aspen down, and our child plopped to the ground, chubby white legs folded under her butt, and buried her face in the carpet, arms above her head like a prayerful monk. Then she let out a hopeless cry. Our older two children, Tristan and Norah, were both sitting on the sofa in the living room still wearing their school uniforms—red shirts with khaki shorts—quietly watching *Pokémon*.

Mel and I were arguing, Aspen was screaming, and Tristan and Norah were hypnotized. Their focus was 100 percent on the TV, and they were paying us zero attention. Nonparents often criticize parents for allowing children to watch so much TV. They don't get it, and it's in moments like these that TV is the spring of life. Mel and I needed to discuss something, one child was crying, and if another child got into the mix, it would've capsized the ship.

Nonparents often criticize parents for allowing children to watch so much TV. They don't get it, and it's in moments like these that TV is the spring of life.

"You've had a long day?" Mel scoffed. "You got to get out of the house. You didn't have to deal with this kid throwing fits all day." She went on, listing messes and nastiness and meltdowns and all the other stresses that come with caring for a toddler.

Mel and I had been through a few different arrangements by this time. We'd both worked. She'd been a stay-at-home mom for a time. I'd been a stay-at-home dad. At various times we'd been in and out of school. At this time, we were dealing with another shift, with Mel staying home with our daughter while our older two were in school. She'd finished her degree, but hadn't found work yet. Each time we'd had a transition like this, it was always a little chaotic, and it was always the worst when we had a toddler because they just don't care if both parents need a break.

"No," I said. "I didn't." Then I went on, telling her about my student who was facing prison time and how stressful that was.

"I'm sure you got a lunch break," she said. "I didn't even get that."

"No. I didn't," I said. "I'm surprised I made it home for dinner."

Neither of us was at our best, and as we were arguing, I failed to notice how quiet it was. Aspen wasn't crying anymore. I didn't know where she was. Nor did I really think much about that at the time because Mel and I were arguing, which was a rookie move. She'd obviously wandered off somewhere in our small, rural Oregon home.

Sometimes it felt like the universe was out of balance when we had a toddler. There should be time to hang out, take a break, take a breath. But it doesn't work that way, so one of us had to suck it up.

Mel and I went back and forth, both attempting to argue that our day had been the worst and, therefore, that each of us was the one justified in taking a break. Both our days had been equally bad, and we were both due a break—but only one could take it. We didn't have family around, and our older two children weren't old enough to be trusted to watch Aspen. Mel or I had to watch her at all times, and there's something maddening about that when everyone is stretched thin. One of us was going to have to suck it up and care for the toddler, but who was it going to be?

Sometimes it felt like the universe was out of balance when we had a toddler. There should be time to hang out, take a break, take a breath. But it doesn't work that way, so one of us had to suck it up. But I didn't want to. It felt like someone owed me something, but who? Aspen was innocent, so she obviously didn't. I felt the same way about my older two children. So I ended up directing those feelings toward my wife. She should know me better than anyone, I reasoned, so why didn't she understand how tired I was? How difficult my day was?

> Aspen had taken off her heavy, pee-soaked diaper. She'd carried it back into the living room and now held it by one strap with both hands, arms stretched out, and was spinning circles with it.

Right?

I knew Mel felt the exact same way.

We'd both earned a moment alone, but neither of us wanted to give it to the other.

Tristan and Norah started screaming.

In the back room, Aspen had taken off her heavy, pee-soaked diaper. She'd carried it back into the living room and now held it by one strap with both hands, arms stretched out, and was spinning circles with it, stumbling around the living room and banging it into the bookshelf and the sofa and the TV . . . basically contaminating everything with toddler pee. Tristan and Norah were on the back of the sofa now, both laughing and cheering.

Aspen was naked, pounding her little legs in circles, blue eyes bright and alive, a huge gummy smile across her face.

Mel and I stopped.

Our argument didn't matter anymore. For a moment, we were a team. We circled her on both sides, arms outstretched like a couple of farmers herding cattle, trying to not be hit by the diaper but failing. We each took a few whacks from the thing on our pant legs before Mel finally grasped Aspen under the armpits to stop her spinning. I grabbed her wrists and yanked the diaper out of her hands. Tristan and Norah sighed in the background, and Aspen started to cry again. Mel picked her up and bounced her. I disposed of the diaper and got a new one. Mel put Aspen on the floor, and both of us got on our knees, Mel holding her down as she cried while I changed her.

For a moment, Mel and I made eye contact, and I let out a half-exhausted laugh and said, "That was unexpected." Mel laughed too, and I don't know what it was about the chaos of those few seconds that seemed to knock something loose, but it did.

Suddenly we did something neither of us wanted to do. We slid into our roles as mother and father like they were winter coats on a summer day.

I picked up Aspen, bounced her, got her calm, got her dressed. Then I had the two older kids clean the table and start their homework. Mel worked on dinner, and once things were truly settled, we set the table together.

A few moments later, we were all eating. Mel and I were able to think a bit more clearly with the fog of toddler-induced temporary insanity behind us. We were on the same team again.

Mel looked at me and said, "I'm sorry to hear about your student."

"Yeah," I said. "Me too. I'm sorry Aspen was a psycho today. That kid's a lot."

Mel shrugged and said, "She's two."

It was quiet for a moment.

Then we discussed who would take the first break.

"The Hardest Part Is Keeping Them Alive"

It was 2009, and I was walking in front of a hotel with my two-year-old son, Tristan. We were staying in southern Utah, attending a Shakespearean festival with my in-laws. I was outside the hotel, trying to keep Tristan quiet so Mel could sleep.

I was holding Tristan's right hand when his legs, feet, arms, chest, head, all of it went limp, like he always did when I told him he couldn't do something.

I felt a pop in his arm.

He was checking out a flowerbed at the time. The sprinklers came on, and I think he wanted to stick his face in the water, or maybe he wanted to drink the water, or perhaps he just wanted to jump in the water, or chase the water, or be the water. I don't know what he wanted to do; he was two, so it was pretty difficult to gauge. I told him we needed to go inside. I told him his mother was waiting for him.

Nothing was good enough, naturally, so he went boneless.

The pop wasn't grotesque or anything. His arm didn't bend in the wrong direction, but I could tell that something wasn't right because, well, the screaming.

He screamed long and hard and deep, his little face bright red. There were people in the parking lot in front of the hotel, and they looked at me as though I'd just beaten him, but I hadn't.

I swear I hadn't.

I was just holding his hand.

I wanted to explain myself to each of them. I wanted to tell them it was an accident. "I didn't mean to hurt him. I'm innocent."

> There was something about caring for a young child that made me feel like I was always on trial. It made me feel like my job was to just keep him alive.

I blamed myself, like all parents do in a situation like this. There was something about caring for a young child that made me feel like I was always on trial. It made me feel like my job was to just keep him alive. And honestly, how hard could that be? Well . . . harder than I could imagine. I was working with a fully mobile little boy who was faster than any Olympian, had no common sense or fear or understanding of harm or death, and would do anything, including bust his own arm, to play with a sprinkler.

I was twenty-four and a new father, so I naturally assumed that I'd permanently injured him. Up until that point Tristan seemed very durable, always falling and getting back up. However, I had a deep fear that I was going to somehow kill him. This was my first, most prominent fear as the parent of a toddler. Before having Tristan, it seemed like I was bombarded with tragic stories of children who'd been lost as a result of what appeared to me, a nonparent, as simple parental errors. But once I got into the game, I realized it wasn't that simple. Caring for my two-year-old son felt like putting pants on someone while they peed in my face and fought desperately to jump in front of a truck.

> However, I had a deep fear that I was going to somehow kill him. This was my first, most prominent fear as the parent of a toddler.

Most days I felt like an impostor.

I wasn't the greatest teenager. I got into some stupid trouble now and again. When hearing that my wife was pregnant, more than one of my friends said, "Are you sure it's legal for you to have children?" They'd raise their eyebrows and then mention something stupid I did once (or twice, or three times) several years prior. It was always said jokingly, but there were moments I anticipated a government agency would swing by and tell me I wasn't qualified to be a father. Anything that might prove my lack of qualifications felt like it was confirming what I'd always suspected—and what others had suspected about me.

This was part of the reason we used to keep Tristan on one of those toddler leashes—because he was kind of a maniac. It was the only way to keep him from being that child who jumped into the tiger cage. It was the only way to keep him from jumping off that bridge and into the river on our family's walking route. It was the only way to keep him from running into traffic at the grocery store. I wanted to keep the little tyke alive, sure, but there was a part of me that knew, without a shadow of a doubt, that if my child ever did run afoul while under my care that I'd be blamed by *all* of the internet, which would only make the tragedy more painful. It would be trending news: "Child Runs into Parking Lot, Suffers Serious Injuries, Parents Blamed for Being Neglectful Losers Who Didn't Care about Their Child and Ultimately Should Be Left to Die on a Raft in the Indian Ocean." Okay, that's a really long headline, but you get the point.

We were still outside the hotel. I looked at Tristan, his right arm limp against his adorable denim coveralls, tears streaming down his face and onto his red fire truck T-shirt, and I felt a rush of anxiety. I was pretty sure I hadn't killed him, so it was easy to check that box. But the final two fears of permanently injuring him and having my son taken away for neglect sat heavy on me.

I cradled him in my arms and took him into the hotel as he screamed the whole time and every person along the way looked at me like I was human garbage.

> This was part of the reason we used to keep Tristan on one of those toddler leashes–because he was kind of a maniac. It was the only way to keep him from being that child who jumped into the tiger cage.

But to be perfectly honest, I don't know if I was actually facing that much judgment. Yes, people were looking at me, but did they really think I'd done something wrong? Did they really think I was unfit to be a parent? Who knows? I'll bet many of them just assumed that I was a young father trying to care for his son, who had obviously had an accident. But in chaos like that, it was difficult to tell all those eyes apart or figure out what they really thought, so it just felt like a reflection of my own shame.

Mel was out of bed and doing her hair once I got to the hotel room. It was one of those middle-ground hotels, with two queen beds and a little refrigerator. It had a couch, which made us feel big-time; but we also got a free continental breakfast, which made it feel like a bargain.

I brought Tristan in and sat him down on the bed. When he saw Mel, he lifted his left arm and it was clear that he wanted to lift his right, but it hurt too much to do so. And when I saw that, I felt this deep mixture of sympathy and fear. He was so little and sweet, with his misty blue eyes and auburn hair, his cheeks rosy red from crying. It felt like he shouldn't have to feel pain and like it was my job to keep him from ever feeling pain—yet there he was, in agony, and here I was, failing at my job.

"What happened?" Mel asked, her hair pulled up on one side lopsidedly, half of it in a clip.

I told her about Tristan going limp when I tried to get him to come inside. I told her about the pop, and how I was pretty sure I'd broke him forever. "He might now have to go through life with a prosthetic, or something," I said. I rambled on for a while until Mel put up her hand and calmly, sweetly told me, "Shut up."

"I have no idea what to do," I said.

Thinking back, what to do seemed obvious. Take Tristan to the doctor. But I'd never had to take him to the doctor for anything other than a regular checkup or a cold or the flu. We didn't have very good insurance; I was still in college. I was worried about how much taking a child to an out-of-network doctor would cost. I'd never done that, and I didn't really understand how it worked.

I was also afraid that the doctor wouldn't believe my story for one reason or another and I'd be put on trial, which would lead to Tristan being taken away. In hindsight, all of this seems very paranoid and crazy, but whenever one of my children has been hurt, I find myself in a stew of emotions and it's always difficult to act rationally. Over the years and with each new child, I've gotten better at handling situations like this. But right then, as a new father, I was more or less in another dimension emotionally, and I'm kind of surprised Mel didn't slap me in the face and scream, "Act like a man!"

Mel sat on the bed and held Tristan, and he eventually calmed down. Then she said, "Let's call a nurse."

"We can do that?" I asked.

She looked at me with a half-twisted lip like I'd been living in a hole, let out an exasperated breath, and said, "Yeah. There's a number on the back of our insurance card."

I took out my wallet, and sure enough . . .

I called and explained things to the nurse. As I did, Tristan began to stomp around the room, acting fine (even laughing a little), aside from his right arm hanging limply at his side like he was an extra in a zombie film. The nurse told me that Tristan probably dislocated his elbow, an injury known as nursemaid's elbow.

"It's very common," she said. "You will probably need to bring him into an urgent care—they should be able to pop it back in."

I later discovered that nursemaid's elbow is indeed a common injury among toddlers. My son would go on to pop his elbow out of alignment a dozen more times, until I felt like we should be getting some sort of a punch card at the doctor's office ("Get your tenth visit free!"). Anything from his going limp while I held his hands, to tripping and falling at the playground, to rolling over in an awkward way caused it. And all I could do was take the kid to see a doctor and have them pop it back in. Eventually it became a normal part of our lives.

The nurse was giving me directions to the nearest urgent care when Tristan tripped over my foot, fell on his right shoulder, and started crying again. I told the nurse to hold on for a moment, the whole time wondering what else I'd just broken on my son. Mel picked him back up, and suddenly he could use his right arm again. He started laughing and grabbing at things in the hotel room.

I told the nurse what happened, and she casually said, "That's great. Sounds like he popped it back in."

I was happy that the problem fixed itself, but I couldn't help but think about that line in *National Lampoon's Christmas Vacation*: "She falls in a well, eyes go crossed. She gets kicked by a mule, they go back to normal. I don't know."

Suddenly I was as good a parent as Uncle Eddie, a man who emptied his RV sewage in the city storm drain.

And right then, I confided in the nurse. I don't know if I was searching for her approval or just trying to make myself not sound like a crappy father, but I told her how embarrassed I was. "I feel like a terrible parent," I said. "I mean, I'm trying. I love the kid. Am I doing it all wrong?"

I held the phone to my ear with my right hand. My left was supporting my face, both elbows on my knees, body hunched in a half-fetal position. I was looking at the ground when the nurse let out a forced, awkward laugh, and I couldn't tell if I'd crossed some nurse-patient line or if this was something she heard all the time. She was quiet for a moment, then she said something that really stuck with me.

"I've been a parent for a long time. And I talk to a lot of nervous parents. It's not easy taking care of little kids. Sometimes they are like a ball bouncing around the room, and all you can do is catch them. And even when you do, they can still get hurt. The hardest part is keeping them alive." She paused for a moment. Then she said, "You're clearly worried about his well-being. That says a lot. I'm sure you're doing just fine."

I got a little choked up, I'll admit, and I couldn't tell if it was from the relief of knowing that Tristan was okay or if it was because of what she'd said.

Perhaps it was both.

"Thank you," I said. "I needed that."

She laughed and said, "Anytime."

Sometimes Getting Up in the Night Was the Only Chance I Had to Feel Like a Dad

I was twenty-four when my mother asked, "Why are you getting up in the night? That's your wife's job."

I was a full-time college student and nearly a full-time server at Olive Garden. Mel worked full-time at Home Depot. Our son spent five days a week with my mother-in-law. We had a lot going on.

My mom and I were talking over the phone. I was complaining to her about how little sleep I'd gotten the night before. She was in her midfifties at the time. I was a little shocked by her question. Mom's a strong woman who was abandoned by my father when I was nine years old. He later died as a result of drug addiction. She raised three children as a single mother. I'd assumed she'd be proud to have a son who was willing to get up in the night, but I was wrong.

I didn't really know how to answer her question, so I said, "I don't know. I just do."

She let out a grunt that seemed to say, *You need to let her know who's the boss.*

I was shocked, but not necessarily by what she said.

The crazy thing is that I never once thought of it as Mel's job versus my job or a gender-roles sort of thing. Don't get me wrong, getting up in the night sucked, but at the same time there was something pretty special about those late-night moments.

And yes, I hate that I just wrote that, and those of you in the midst of the sleep fight are probably rolling your bloodshot eyes reading it. But hold on for just a moment more. I can explain.

We tried not letting him nap during the day, which sucked worse than I could've imagined. It felt like I was trying to run a sleepless marathon while holding a screaming human.

When Tristan was a baby, he'd sleep only if someone sat up and cradled him in one arm, like a football. I'd like to say I was pretty good at falling asleep while holding him, but that'd be a lie. I mean,

I sometimes drifted off, but most of the night was a fog in which I slid in and out of sleep, the TV on in the living room.

As Tristan got older, well into his twos, he didn't get any better. We tried everything we could think of to get that kid to sleep. We rubbed him down with aromatherapy lotions filled with lavender, chamomile, ylang-ylang (I'm still not exactly sure what that one is), and other scents that were meant to put him down. It made me feel like some amateur masseuse. Every one of these lotions either had the opposite effect, because rubbing them on the kid made him giggle and pepped him up, or no effect at all outside of making me drowsier than I was before while making our toddler as slippery as a dolphin.

We tried not letting him nap during the day, which sucked worse than I could've imagined. It felt like I was trying to run a sleepless marathon while holding a screaming human. We waited until he looked drowsy and tried to quickly drop everything and get him to bed, which more or less meant turning off dinner or forgoing a college assignment so that one of us could fight a squirmy turd of a child in the hopes that he'd fall asleep, only for him to gaze back at us with wide-open eyes.

What frustrated me the most about these useless sleep tactics was that the parents who recommended them pledged that they worked wonders. And every time I used one and they didn't work,

I wondered if there was something wrong with Tristan.

The only way to get the little boy to sleep was to play *Baby Einstein: Lullaby Time* on repeat, clear out the room, and hold him on the couch for a good hour. Sometimes it took longer. The lullaby movie was a mix of random toys and repetitive images mixed to soothing classical songs, and sometimes I'd be up so long with that toddler it felt like I was on an acid trip and that random, pilotless movie started to make sense: "The train moves in a circle. I get it now." I'd set Tristan on my lap so he could see the TV. Each time he tried to crawl down, I'd tug him back, and he'd say, "I stuck. I stuck," all of it feeling very *A Clockwork Orange*.

Then Tristan would wake up after an hour or two, and I'd drive him around town in the dark, lullabies on the CD player, Tristan strapped into his car seat and smiling up at me with his two-toothed grin, legs kicking. I'd look at him through the rearview mirror, wondering if there was some way for me to slip into a coma that lasted until Tristan was old enough to sleep through the night.

Sometimes he'd cry in his crib, and I'd get up and hold him. He'd fight and wiggle then insist we play a game he called "I'm going to get you," in which I'd give him a head start and he'd hide in the kitchen of our small farm home in Provo, Utah. He always hid in this four-foot gap between the refrigerator and the dishwasher, and every time

I caught him, he'd act all surprised. It might be midnight, it might be 4:00 a.m., it didn't matter—we were playing that stupid game.

One of my professors pulled me aside after class one time and asked a few questions about my lifestyle and mental health, which, more or less, circled around the idea that I might be partying too hard or suffering from narcolepsy.

"Nope," I said. "I just have a toddler."

He was a father of five, so he just nodded and said, "I'm sorry."

For more than two years, Mel and I split the night in half. I fell asleep in classes and in the university hallways. If I didn't have a table at Olive Garden, I'd hide in the storeroom, where they kept the fountain drink pouches and extra breadsticks and fall asleep sitting on a bucket, my head resting against a bag of flour.

Sometimes I fell asleep on the bus and woke up in strange places.

One of my professors pulled me aside after class one time and asked a few questions about my lifestyle and mental health, which, more or less, circled around the idea that I might be partying too hard or suffering from narcolepsy.

"Nope," I said. "I just have a toddler."

He was a father of five, so he just nodded and said, "I'm sorry."

I couldn't imagine placing this responsibility solely on Mel. She was as tired as I was, stumbling around her job at the Home Depot, sleeping in the break room or drifting off next to the potted plants in the back of the greenhouse, slapping herself in the face with each commute.

But you know what? As I'm writing this, I cannot help but smile when thinking back on those late-night moments with my son.

Yes, I was exhausted.

Yes, it sucked.

As much as I hated it, being up in the night provided me with some of the only memories I have of spending time with my son during his toddler years.

About five years after my mother asked me why I got up in the night, I was just out of graduate school and working at a university. I had a white-collar education but earned a blue-collar wage. I was an academic counselor at a traditional brick-and-mortar university; sometimes I also taught at that same university, and I taught two, sometimes three, classes at a time for an online university.

I got up early, and when papers were in, I came home late. Some days I didn't see my kids.

Mel was busy too. She was a full-time mom of a five- and three-year-old, and a part-time student.

I'd sometimes come home late to find her in sweat-pants, hunching over a keyboard, eyes bloodshot, and both children asleep on the sofa, a movie on the TV.

It was around this time that I was chatting with my mother over the phone again. She asked how I was doing, and I told her I was tired. I told her about getting up in the night because Norah wasn't all that much better of a sleeper than Tristan was. And she said the same thing she had years ago, when I was a new father.

"Getting up in the night is your wife's job."

We didn't speak for a minute.

I let out a breath and told her what I wished I'd said the first time she asked: "Sometimes, Mom, getting up in the night is the only chance I get to feel like a father."

I told her about my long hours at work. Then I told her about how the night was sometimes the only chance I had to solve my kids' problems, to hold them for a moment, or to hear the sweet words, "I love you, Daddy." I told her about the way Tristan, then five years old, tightly gripped my arm when I sat in bed with him after a nightmare. I told her about then three-year-old Norah, curled up in a crying, shivering ball at 2:00 a.m. and how satisfied I felt after seeing her stretch out beneath the warm quilt I laid over her.

In those moments, I felt needed.

I felt valued.

She didn't respond for a moment. I could hear her breathing on the other line. Then she said, "Those are some pretty good reasons to get up in the night."

"Exactly," I said. "Exactly."

Hell Is Taking a Two-Year-Old on a Plane

We were in the security line at the Minneapolis–Saint Paul airport, flying to Utah to see family. Our two-year-old, Tristan, was holding Mel's hand, and our nearly one-year-old daughter, Norah, was in the stroller. It was the summer after my first year of graduate school, and Mel and I were excited to see family for the first time in what felt like eons. But we'd never flown with a toddler; so, like idiots, we took an early flight with a connection in Denver in hopes of saving money. I can't remember exactly what time it was, but it was still dark outside. We lived an hour and a half away from the airport, so it felt like we'd gotten up before God created the earth to catch that flight.

We had two car seats, multiple outfits, enough diapers and wipes for a year, tons of formula, snacks to feed an army of toddlers, a portable DVD player, and a number of coloring books. Mel packed it all in four carry-on luggage bags and a stroller with the brilliance of an engineer.

We stood before a dark blue TSA podium, where a bald, mustached, slightly pudgy agent was checking our IDs. Mel and I were both crisscrossed with luggage bags like a couple of Sherpas on Mount Everest, Norah was sleeping in the stroller, and Tristan was tugging at my pant leg, asking to be held, red-faced and moody from lack of sleep. But between handling IDs and bags and car seats and the stroller, neither Mel nor I had a free hand, so Tristan fell down and screamed into the carpet. I glanced behind us at the massive line, and I felt confident that if those people had had stones they would've thrown them, because we were obviously holding things up. Once I finally got a free hand, I crouched down and dragged Tristan into my right arm, his body limp with dramatics, every ounce of him dead weight.

We took off our shoes, jackets, belts, the usual. Then we did the same for Tristan while also dismantling our stroller and waking Norah. We placed everything in an endless line on the X-ray conveyor belt, and there was this awkward, tense moment where the agent crammed one of our car seats into the machine with the same force one might use when stuffing a garbage can. As he pushed it in, I had this terrifying realization that if somehow that sucker got jammed, our whole family would be killed by an angry mob of angsty, bloodthirsty airplane passengers who were fearful that we'd just come between them and their flight.

Norah was crying, so Mel bounced her as agents went through our bags and removed most of our snacks. According to the airport's website, they all were approved carry-on items, but I didn't argue with the agent because behind us were literally a hundred people wondering if we actually needed all these things to fly with children, and in front of me was Tristan crouching down, lips in a flat line, eyebrows furrowed, face red. "I . . . am . . . pooping!" he said.

I ended up handling Tristan's butt on a men's room changing table that felt sticky with the germs of many nations. It was a blowout, naturally, and suddenly we were down one diaper, several wipes, and an outfit.

Mel and I made our usual eye contact, trying to decide who would handle our poopy toddler in the airport. And by the time all of our belongings were through security and repacked and our shoes and belts were back on our bodies and Tristan was as ripe as a compost pile, Mel was giving Norah a bottle. I ended up handling Tristan's butt on a men's room changing table that felt sticky with the germs of many nations. It was a blowout, naturally, and suddenly we were down one diaper, several wipes, and an outfit.

Since we were now low on snacks, thanks to the TSA, we stopped in a newsstand and more or less exchanged Tristan's college fund for a bag of fruit snacks and a half-tube of potato chips. Then we sprinted across the airport to catch our first flight. It was then that I discovered a universal truth: Airports cause a two-year-old's legs to stop working. I somehow managed to carry Tristan, along with the luggage and a car seat, for what felt like forty years, and by the time we made it to the tarmac, I just wanted to die.

But there wasn't really time for that.

I swear to you, there was a collective sigh from passengers as we boarded.

The last call for boarding went overhead as our tickets were scanned. I wobbled onto the plane, Tristan in my arms, Norah in Mel's, our many bags smacking each seat as we passed. I swear to you, there was a collective sigh from passengers as we boarded. They probably assumed that no one on this flight had children. But their grief wasn't nearly as obvious as the looks of horror from the fifteen or so people closest to our seats. Once we got settled, Norah sleeping on Mel's chest and Tristan sitting on my lap, his million-dollar newsstand snacks in his chubby little hands, there was a quiet, peaceful moment as the plane taxied onto the runway. I naively looked at Mel and said, "We made it."

I even winked.

She smiled back at me as the plane took off.

But we hadn't really "made" anything.

We were still very much in hell.

The wheels left the runway, startling Tristan and causing him to spill his snacks. I swear to you, I saw dollar signs escaping, similar to when a *Harry Potter* Dementor sucks out a wizard's soul. Then he tugged at his ear and cried because it wouldn't pop. We tried to show him how to move his jaw or yawn, but he wouldn't do any of it. Mel gave him some gum, but he was too upset to place it in his mouth.

Ultimately, it was his own screaming that did the trick.

The moment the seat belt sign turned off, Tristan grunted, then looked back at me and smiled.

He'd pooped again.

I felt the rumble in my lap.

Norah was sleeping on Mel, so I carried Tristan to the airplane restroom, the diaper bag over my shoulder. Once inside it felt like I'd entered a coffin. There was no way for me to lay him down, so I had to change him standing up on the toilet seat. I'd just wiped him clean when he pushed the button to flush the toilet. The sound scared him so badly he peed before I got the clean diaper on. I used wipes on Tristan, the restroom, and myself. To get everything clean I had to twist, arch, and stretch in ways I never had before. By the time I was done, I felt confident that I could list "yoga master" on my resume.

The flight attendant gave Tristan a half-cup of juice, and the kid handled it like a drunken woman in heels handles a martini.

Tristan pooped one more time during the flight, and Mel had the pleasure of handling it this time. She was gone for what seemed like far longer than I expected, and once she came back, Tristan was in a third outfit. Mel's once-tight ponytail had several loose strands, and she had a pale look of exhausted panic, a little sweat on her forehead. When I asked her how it went, she just looked forward and said, "I don't want to talk about it."

The flight attendant gave Tristan a half-cup of juice, and the kid handled it like a drunken woman in heels handles a martini. I used wipes on that mess too. We brought books, crayons, and movies. Nothing. They did nothing. Tristan just wanted to hit me with the seat belt and ask for candy, so I gave it to him . . . so much candy, anything to keep him calm. Which worked, I'll admit, until we started our descent and he threw up, an act that ultimately solidified our status as the most popular family on the plane.

We made it to Denver and discovered our flight to Salt Lake City had been delayed by two hours. We also accepted the fact that Tristan had a full-blown case of diarrhea. Diapers, outfits, and wipes were almost gone, and after asking every single vendor, I came to the realization that the Denver airport didn't sell diapers because they hate parents, and children, and want to see the world burn.

By the time we boarded our next flight, we were out of diapers and outfits and had to buy Tristan new clothes at the airport. The options were limited. Tristan boarded that flight in a Denver Broncos T-shirt and matching sweatpants, and beneath it all was a Colorado State University hand towel held at his hips with a few staples.

I wondered if connecting flights with a two-year-old was comparable to competing in an Ironman.

I should probably admit that the second leg of our trip wasn't quite as bad as the first. Tristan was all out of poop and not feeling well, so he slept most of the flight. However, I would also like it to be noted that by the time we landed in Salt Lake, I realized I'd been sweating profusely, and I wondered if connecting flights with a two-year-old was comparable to competing in an Ironman. I know this sounds like an exaggeration, but I once read an article about a medical study that found toddlers are as fit as endurance athletes. Be sure to mention that the next time your doctor asks if you exercise regularly.

I was exhausted, yet somehow I managed to muster up the strength to keep Tristan from climbing onto the baggage carousel.

Once we had our luggage, car seats, and stroller and we were safely inside my in-laws' van, I promised myself I'd never fly with a toddler again— but I knew, somehow, that it was unavoidable.

If I go to hell, it will be flying with a two-year-old for eternity.

Just before pulling away from the airport, my father-in-law turned around in the driver's seat and asked, "How was your flight?"

Neither of us answered. Mel and I just looked at him with cold, dead eyes.

Let's Take a Trip to the Emergency Room

We were in the emergency room because my two-year-old daughter burned her hand on oven-baked mashed potatoes. It was 2010. Norah was whimpering on my lap, her small hand red and blistered, short brown hair curling just a bit on the end, face soft and red and heartbreaking.

Across from me was a forty-something brown-haired nurse wearing glasses and blue scrubs. I was holding Norah's burned hand out for her to examine, but the little girl was fighting me, and I couldn't tell if she was afraid the nurse would hurt her more or if she just didn't want to show a stranger what had happened. I don't know exactly what was going through her head. What I can say is that I felt deep sorrow in the pit of my stomach when I looked at her small blistering hand, and I had a difficult time fully understanding that emotion.

Two hours before we visited the hospital, we were about to have dinner as a family. I spent all day with the family on Sundays. This was a new thing.

Mel and I were in our midtwenties. We'd been married about six years. I was in graduate school, and between classes, teaching, and had side work with a small children's publisher, I didn't have much time for dinner with the family. Is that the right phrase? "Have time"? I suppose what I should say is that I didn't make time.

> Hanging out with my toddler-age daughter and son wasn't exactly my idea of a good time. They smelled funny, they tugged at me and drooled on me, they threw fits and got in fights, and all of it was simply uncomfortable.

And to be honest, at the time it didn't bother me too much. There were a couple reasons for this.

Hanging out with my toddler-age daughter and son wasn't exactly my idea of a good time. They smelled funny, they tugged at me and drooled on me, they threw fits and got in fights, and all of it was simply uncomfortable. So I went to work. I went to school. I spent long swaths of time in the restroom.

I also didn't fully understand what "family" really meant.

Not that I didn't understand the dictionary definition of "mother," "father," "son," "daughter." I got that. I also understood it in a legal sense. I understood that Mel and I had an obligation to pay *all* the medical bills, and school bills, and food bills, and everything else that came at us as parents. But I didn't really understand the importance of time with the family, because I didn't have a great relationship with *my* parents.

I know, I know. I read what I just wrote and it sounds like a daytime talk show confession, but it's true. My father left when I was nine. My mother was married three times, and my father died divorcing his fourth wife. As a child, I bounced between my mother, father, and grandmother. I have a slew of stepsiblings who came in and out of my life. I once tried to introduce my former stepsister to Mel via Facebook, and I suddenly didn't know what to call her. It was so strange to have worn a boutonniere at her wedding, shared holidays and graduations with her, and then suddenly not have a name for our relationship.

Family had always seemed like a temporary thing, and that really came out in graduate school.

About two weeks before Norah burned her hand, Mel sat down at the kitchen table where I was reading a book for one of my classes and asked, "When was the last time you had dinner with us?"

I scoffed. "Not that long ago." I was in a red button-up shirt and black slacks (my teaching clothes). I paused for a moment, deep in thought. "It was like . . ." I paused again.

Mel was in pajama pants and a T-shirt. It was evening. The kids were in bed. She looked me in the eyes, never wavering as I tried to answer. There was one light above the stove. It was a dull light, and it was to my back so I could still see my book without bothering the kids. It was in Mel's face now.

"One day," she said as she held up her right index finger. "You will give us one day, or I'm done. I can't do this alone."

I let out a breath and reluctantly agreed.

Norah burned her hand on the second Sunday I spent with the family. Mel was trying a new recipe for buttery baked mashed potatoes. They cooked at 450 degrees. Mel set the pan of potatoes on the table then scooped some into a bowl so they could cool. Norah was in the high chair. Mel set everything on the opposite side of the table, well out of reach. Norah stretched out for the potatoes, and Tristan, her doting older brother, slid the bowl across the table to his little sister.

Mel and I both saw it happen, and we both lunged forward—but not fast enough.

Norah stuck her hand into the bowl. She let out a long cry and held out her hand.

I could tell when Norah cried for attention. I

could tell when she cried because of injustice, and I knew when she cried because of a scuffed knee. But I'd never heard anything quite like the way Norah cried after burning her hand. It was both deep and high. It was filled with panic and sorrow. It was a mixture of tones and pitches, and it set off something inside me that I couldn't explain. Never in my life have I wanted so badly to reach inside and take away someone's pain.

Mel called a nurse hotline and they suggested we rinse Norah's hand in warm water. But she still cried. I held her body next to the sink as Mel held her hand under the water and we both watched the skin bubble.

It was then that we took Norah to the emergency room.

This was our first visit to the ER with a child. At the time, I recall assuming that Tristan would be the first to make a visit. He was the rambunctious boy in the family; but instead it was Norah, our chubby-faced, soft-mannered little girl.

We were in the waiting room for some time, with Norah in my lap, snuggled into my chest, whimpering, her hand folded down into a hook shape. It was bright red and sad, and by the time we made it to the actual emergency room, I was a mess of emotions. I wondered if her hand would be permanently scarred. I wondered how long her recovery would be. I worried about her like I'd never worried about anyone in my life.

I told our story to the nurse in "um's" and "oh's." I overexplained and asked a lot of questions as I spoke. I was a nervous wreck.

The nurse listened. She told us things like, "This happens." She told a story of when her young son was burned on a fireplace. She tried to make us feel comfortable.

A doctor came in. He had dark, thinning hair and a large round gut. He examined the hand, held it up into the light so he could see it better, and recommended it be cleaned, covered with ointment, and wrapped. He said Norah would heal in a few weeks.

Nothing serious.

Then the nurse had me hold out Norah's small, tender fist so she could clean it and cover it in burn cream. Tristan sat watching in a chair. Mel had one arm around me and the other around Norah, her head against my shoulder.

I couldn't remember the last time I'd cried. But there, in that emergency room, as the nurse treated my two-year-old daughter's burned hand, I cried.

The nurse scrubbed her hand, and Norah let out the same deep, horrible cry she did when the accident first happened. Her whole body trembled in my lap, and I felt something horrible and weighty in my gut. It was a mixture of sorrow, regret, frustration, and anger, and it felt like a ball of heat crawling into my throat. Once it got there, it rested just below my jaw.

I didn't cry when my father walked out. I didn't cry when my parents divorced. I didn't cry when my father died. I didn't cry when I got married or when my children were born. I couldn't remember the last time I'd cried. But there, in that emergency room, as the nurse treated my two-year-old daughter's burned hand, I cried.

And once it was all over, Norah's hand wrapped in a mitten of white gauze, her sleeping soundly on my chest, my shirt still wet with tears, I felt a deep connection with that little girl I'd never felt with anyone else—family or otherwise—and I felt deep relief knowing that the worst of it was over for her.

How I Plan to Get Revenge on My Toddlers Once They Are Adults

When I got married, my mother said she planned to come to my home, turn my ceiling fan on high, and throw toys into it. Or pull all the toilet paper off the roll and drag it down the hallway, laughing. Or wipe boogers on the walls. Or, well, basically all the things I did as a kid. Why? Revenge. She said it jokingly, and I always gave it an epic eye roll. Then I had children of my own, and now, well, I get it.

There's something about my kids pushing all my buttons that makes me long for revenge once they are adults. Sure, I'll never do it. But it is fun to imagine all the ways I'd love to get even so they will understand exactly how awesome I was as a parent. Here are a few examples that are not in any particular order (all would be equally satisfying means of revenge):

1. Hide in my daughter's pantry and crap my pants.

2. Punch my son in the balls while shopping at Target. Then laugh in his face.

3. Leave a leaky sippy cup full of milk under the back seat of their car for an entire summer.

4. Knock on my son's door moments before he is about to have sex and tell him I want to change my pajamas.

5. Wake them up at 4:00 a.m. and ask for a cheese stick every day until they wake up at 4:00 a.m. on their own for the rest of their lives.

6. Poop my pants on my son's nicest piece of furniture.

7. Loudly argue with my son while grocery shopping about whether he can smell my fart.

8. Walk naked into my daughter's living room while it is full of guests, then get offended when I'm asked to get dressed.

9. Walk in on my son while he's changing his underwear, point at his crotch, and laugh.

10. Poop in the tub and ask them to fish it out.

11. Urinate on a tree in my son's backyard while he is hosting a family reunion barbecue.

12. Make it rain granola in their cars.

13. Sprawl out on their new sofa with dog crap on my shoes.

14. Cry until they take me to McDonald's, then place a booger on my tongue and show it to everyone in line.

15. Come over for an amazing Thanksgiving dinner, look at the food as though it were a hate crime, and scream until someone makes me mac and cheese.

16. Crawl into their bed in the middle of the night, sprawl out, kick them in the kidneys periodically, and give them three to four inches of actual bed space so they wake up feeling like they've been in a bar fight.

17. Have my daughter pay for me to stay in the Disneyland Hotel and then cry because the water tastes funny.

18. Scream for someone to come wipe my butt the moment any of them sit down to a hot meal.

19. Pee in my son's restroom like a baby elephant using his trunk to cool off on a hot day in Africa.

20. Pull down my son's swimming suit at the community pool, then cry when he gets mad at me for showing the whole town his doodle.

21. Put the wrong password into their phone 800 million times so that it becomes locked for eternity.

22. Ask them to buy me things until they cry.

23. Shove Silly Putty between their car seats.

24. Shove French fries into the air vents of their cars.

25. Pick a fight in the back seat of the car so the driver has to reach back and break it up. Preferably on the freeway.

26. Throw an empty sippy cup at the driver and
    ask for more milk.

   Are twenty-six revenge tactics enough? I mean,
I could go on. I have so much more. But this is
a good start, I think. And I know, I know. As an
adult, these sorts of things would probably get me
disowned by my children, or worse . . . arrested.
But it sure is fun to think about, isn't it? Sometimes
thinking about revenge was the only thing that got
me through the day with a toddler.

Can We Talk about Hand, Foot, and Mouth for a Moment?

———————————————

I was changing Aspen's diaper when I noticed a bubbly rash on her butt. She was a little squirmy but no more than usual, and I didn't think much of it. Two days later, on Christmas day, she came down with a fever, and the rash spread to her hands, feet, and mouth.

We lived in a small Oregon town, and all of our doctors were in Salem, forty minutes away, and I didn't want to go to Salem to visit a doctor on Christmas. No one does. So I went to WebMD. And I know, I already brought up this website in a previous story, and you'd think I'd have learned my lesson, but—*shrug*—I go to it far too often; which is stupid, considering it once convinced me

I had cancer. I even argued with my doctor about it. Turns out it wasn't cancer. It was a pimple. Probably closer to a boil. Yes, a boil. That sounds closer to cancer. It doesn't matter, because I was proven wrong when the doctor popped it and sent me home with a pretty large bill. And I think right there is where the problem really sits with WebMD. It provides free answers. But what is the cost of free? That, my friends, is a deep philosophical question I can't answer. But I can say that WebMD's free advice, in this particular moment with my daughter, scared the crap out of me.

I put Aspen's info into the Symptom Checker, only to have it list some illnesses I'd heard of—strep throat and West Nile virus, for example—and a number of things I'd never heard of, with terrifying names like septic shock and sepsis (a blood infection). Mel and I looked over the results. We grew more nervous. Aspen got more listless, and eventually Mel decided to take her to the doctor while I stayed at home with Tristan and Norah and finished cooking the Christmas ham.

She'd been gone for a couple hours when I got this text: "She has hand, foot, and mouth disease."

"Isn't that something cows get?" I asked.

"Obviously not," Mel replied.

And like an idiot, I went online . . . again. Turns out hand, foot, and mouth is really common and is not related to foot-and-mouth disease, which is a severe, highly contagious viral disease in cows, pigs, sheep, goats, deer, and other animals with cleft hooves. WebMD didn't have a page on foot-and-mouth disease. I got that information from USDA.gov, which has nothing to do with children and everything to do with farming.

Anyway, among children under eight, nearly two hundred thousand cases of hand, foot, and mouth disease are reported in the United States each year. I found this terrifying and comforting. There was something about the name that made it seem like we'd picked up a strange illness that was a result of not cleaning, or bathing, or some other simple downfall that proved we were bad parents. This happens a lot with me. I often assume that whatever is wrong with my child, from a virus to a broken bone, is a result of some neglectful action on my part.

When I was an undergrad, I had a physics professor tell me about this family who lived next to a nuclear waste storage facility. The place went out of business, so the dad went snooping around the abandoned building, only to find some glow-in-the-dark paint. He put it on the trim in the hallway of his home so his kids could see their way to the bathroom at night. Turns out it wasn't paint but radioactive waste, and the whole family died the next day.

Okay, that was dark, but that dad probably had the best intentions. I, too, have the best intentions. Do you see where I'm going with this? I talk a lot about needing a manual, something I can cross-reference when I'm dealing with potential ailments and that would make me feel better about everything. But there isn't one, so I just get on WebMD and wonder if I'm absentmindedly killing my children.

So yeah, I felt better knowing that hand, foot, and mouth disease was common.

However, I didn't like finding out that it would last for two weeks, that it was very contagious and very painful, and that because it was a virus, there was nothing outside of the recommendation to "get rest" that could be done. According to people online, the rashes would eventually turn into blisters, and the blisters get under the children's fingernails, and then their fingernails fall off.

Aren't we in America? I thought.

This was some horrible and grotesque business, and the thought of my other children getting this virus sounded like total hell.

By the time Mel got home I'd more or less given up on the ham and was shampooing carpet and washing sheets in an attempt to contain the virus. We were supposed to have friends over for Christmas dinner, but I told them about the fingernails and suggested they stay home.

"You don't want this in your house," I said. "This is some third-world stuff."

Mel walked in with Aspen on her hip. The little girl's soft mouth was spackled with red bumps. Her blue eyes were misty, and she kept opening and closing her hands as if they were numb. She looked like she'd been crying, and I wanted to give her a hug; but at the same time, I was afraid to touch her.

I'd been watching *The Man in the High Castle*, an alternate-history drama that explores the question of what life in America would be like if the Nazis had won World War II. One of the torture techniques the SS soldiers used to interrogate prisoners was pulling off their fingernails. Just the thought disturbed my sleep, and the fact that there was a virus that could do something similar to Nazi torture made me wonder if hand, foot, and mouth wasn't a virus at all but the brainchild of biological warfare.

> But with my kids, they could
> have leprosy, or polio, or the freaking
> bubonic plague and I'd be obligated
> to wipe their bleeding rectums and
> help them peel off dead skin.

If Mel had come down with hand, foot, and mouth, I'd have kept my distance. I'd have been compassionate. I'd have cared for the children and made her soup. But I'd have flat-out stopped touching her. Mel would have done the same if the situation were reversed, no doubt about it. But with my kids, they could have leprosy, or polio, or the freaking bubonic plague and I'd be obligated to wipe their bleeding rectums and help them peel off dead skin.

Mel sat Aspen on the kitchen floor and said, "Worst. Christmas. Ever."

Aspen walked to me with a painful strut and tugged at my pant leg. I looked down at her and thought, *Please. Please don't do this to me.*

I wanted to lock her in a room until this was all over. When Tristan was a baby, he came down with some nasty thing that had him gushing out of both ends. I remember getting up in the night to find him reaching up from a quarter inch of fluid—I wanted to turn my back and start over with a new child. But I didn't because I'm a father. So I picked him up, poop and all, same as I did Aspen.

I prayed, silently, that somehow, some way, I'd finish this thing out unscathed with all my fingernails.

This is what unconditional love really looks like . . .

Mel gave me a list of over-the-counter ointments and painkillers the doctor recommended. There were no prescriptions.

"What's this crap?" I said.

Mel rolled her eyes. "It's a virus," she said. "They can't give us anything."

"Couldn't they at least prescribe a placebo?" I said. "Just give me some magic beans, I don't care."

Mel shrugged.

Norah was in the room now. She looked at her sister with a sad tucked-in lip, then reached up and touched Aspen's leg.

"Don't touch her!" I screamed. "She's contagious!"

"I just wanted to give her a hug," Norah said. Then she cried and ran into her room, leaving me feeling like a total butthead.

I spent the rest of the day making trips to Walgreens (the only pharmacy in town open on Christmas day), picking up everything from ointments to replacement toothbrushes, bath toys, shoes, and anything else Aspen might have put in her mouth in the past few days. I felt guilty for shopping on a holiday but also sincerely grateful that someplace in small-town Oregon was open.

The next several nights were the longest of my parenthood. Mel and I took care of Aspen in shifts. Most of the time was spent watching *Blue's Clues* and trying to find a way to hold Aspen and keep her comfortable, which was difficult because her bum, lower back, and upper thighs were covered in bleeding, blistery rashes.

I couldn't have slept more than a few hours for several nights, and I started to hate Blue's buddy Steve, and Magenta, and Blue herself. I started to hate hand, foot, and mouth. I started to hate everything but my daughter, who was ultimately the source of the problem, but because she was my own she had immunity from my hatred.

About three days in, I got Aspen undressed for

a bath and noticed that one of the blisters on her bum was peeling. I pulled on a loose flap of skin and a patch the size of her left butt cheek peeled off. Below was red and raw.

Mel came into the room and stared at the tea saucer–size patch of skin in my hand, her face confused, trying to make sense of it.

"What happened?" she asked.

I shrugged. "It just came off?"

Aspen stood up. She was naked and little and helpless, her blonde hair mashed in the back. She gave me a sad, watery-eyed face like I'd done something personal by peeling off her skin. In my left hand was an orange stuffed cat she received in her Christmas stocking. She ripped it from me, snuggled it, and screamed. She waddled down the hall to the tub, her sad little bum in view, crying the whole way.

She lost a little more skin that night from her hands and feet. But slowly she started to get better. There wasn't some dramatic turning point but more of a progression, and by the end of the next day she started to laugh again.

I was in the living room cleaning up. I was exhausted from being up too many nights, and I'd been back to work for a few days. Mel was in the kitchen making dinner. Our older two were in their rooms.

Aspen was walking around the living room. I made eye contact with her and she grabbed her tummy, leaned her head back almost dramatically, and started laughing. It ended with a funny, sweet giggle, and I crouched down on the floor beside her. She looked at me and laughed again.

Mel came into the room and stared at the tea saucer-size patch of skin in my hand, her face confused, trying to make sense of it.

"What happened?" she asked.

I shrugged. "It just came off?"

I hadn't realized she wasn't laughing before then. She couldn't have been, because once she laughed I noticed what had been missing. The past several days she'd had a few emotional states: angry, listless, sad, sleepy, but not joyful.

I've never fully understood why I get such a thrill out of seeing them smile. But I do. I think all parents do. And when it's gone, it feels like there's a hole somewhere that can't be filled. I think that's the really troubling part of having a sick kid. They don't smile. They don't giggle or play around. They just sit there, sad or mad, and you want so bad to see them happy again.

I reached out and grabbed Aspen by the hips and pulled her next to me. "Looks like you are feeling better."

She responded in gibberish and then laughed again, and I felt warm inside. I gave her a big hug.

No one else in the family came down with the virus. That night, she slept better than the nights before. And the next day she started losing her fingernails. But it wasn't as bad as I thought. She didn't appear to feel any pain from it. After that laugh, she didn't appear to be in pain at all anymore.

That first night after she laughed, I watched her sleep, curled on one side, body in a C shape. Although I didn't do much outside of hold her in the night and give her ointment, I felt a sense of satisfaction as I stood in her bedroom doorway. Sure, she was the sick one, but in a way we both survived something difficult.

I leaned down and kissed her forehead. She squirmed a bit and went back to a deep sleep. I closed her bedroom door and slept better than I had in days.

Forty Real Two-Year-Old Pro Tips

I often read lists of tips to make the two-year-old year easier, and they were always fluffy and full of little tricks that didn't work and made me feel like a failure. Or they made me feel like there was something wrong with my two-year-old, which isn't true. Well, actually, I think there is something wrong with all two-year-olds because, you know . . . two-year-olds. Sometimes I wonder if people without kids write these lists. Anyway, let's bring it down a level, shall we?

Here's a little list of my own. I won't BS you. Here are the real two-year-old pro tips. You're welcome.

1. When on the sofa, be sure to protect your eyes, crotch, face, hair, and breasts. Two-year-olds have surprisingly strong grips.

2. Dinosaur-shaped chicken nuggets are your manna.

3. The best time to play peekaboo is when changing a particularly messy diaper. It keeps a two-year-old from eating it.

4. If a two-year-old eats dirt, technically you don't have to feed them the next meal. Plus, it's organic.

5. You will eventually wake up to your two-year-old standing next to your bed, quietly watching you sleep. It will scare you. Bad. This is not a tip. It's a warning.

6. Give up on shoes. Keeping shoes on a two-year-old is about as easy as keeping shoes on a cat. Put them on in the morning so you feel good about yourself. The rest of the day is in God's hands.

7. One Popsicle will keep a two-year-old content for three minutes. With enough Popsicles, you can load the entire dishwasher without your two-year-old trying to climb inside it.

8. The two-year-old is the boss of you now. You can redirect them some, but ultimately they run the show. Keeping that in mind will help you not feel like a failure the next time you bring the little bugger to Target.

9. You don't have to give your two-year-old a bath every day. Just wipe them down sometimes. Parents who bathe their two-year-old every single day obviously hate themselves.

10. Avoid moving the car seat at all costs. It will only remind you how out of shape you actually are, and you honestly don't want to know what's growing inside it.

11. The easiest way to clean the car seat is with the garden hose.

12. Actually, you know what, don't waste time cleaning the two-year-old's car seat. It's a battle you can't win. Just wait until they grow out of it and light the thing on fire.

13. Bingeing on ice cream can prevent you from becoming an alcoholic.

14. If a two-year-old hands you something, it will be wet. With what? It's best not to know.

15. If you find a long-lost sippy cup, don't open it. Just throw it away. Opening it is like opening the seventh seal.

16. McDonald's is a toddler's Starbucks. It isn't healthy and it's expensive, but it sure makes the day easier on everyone.

17. Wipes can clean everything from butts to counters to car seats. Wipes will be your Swiss Army knife.

18. Sometimes it feels really nice to flip your two-year-old off when their back is turned. Once again, can't find a law on the books for this, so you're good.

19. Don't worry about making sure your two-year-old looks cute all the time. Sometimes it's all you can do to keep their pants on.

20. The shame you feel for using a crayon instead of a pen is not nearly as painful as searching for a pen while holding a two-year-old.

21. A great way to relax is to lie on the floor and let the two-year-old climb on you. But remember tip number 1.

22. Don't buy a two-year-old any clothing with buttons. People who design two-year-olds' clothing with buttons either don't have children or are cage fighters.

23. If you buy a two-year-old a really extravagant birthday gift, they will play with the box. Save money and just buy a box.

24. If your two-year-old's diaper leaks in the night, just change them and throw down a towel. Washing sheets at 3:00 a.m. will make you understand why some animals eat their young.

25. Backyard kids' pools are a wonderful way to spend all day fearing that your two-year-old is about to drown.

26. Arguing with a two-year-old is the first step to failure.

27. Swimming counts as a bath.

28. Once your two-year-old learns how to lock a door, have keys at all times. Two-year-olds don't care (see page 87).

29. If they drop candy on the floor, let them eat it. The dirt makes it organic.

30. Screw pants with a legitimate waist. You don't need that in your life. Jeans and a belt feel like a ball and chain after sleeping only four hours because of your two-year-old.

31. A stash of candy just for you that's hidden in the laundry room will help keep your two-year-old healthy—and help you maintain your sanity.

32. If a two-year-old wants liquid in a cup without a lid, make sure it's water and that all electronics are three feet above the toddler. A two-year-old holding a cup without a lid is basically *Waterworld*.

33. Suffering is taking a two-year-old to the store for a birthday gift that isn't for them, so mentally prepare yourself.

34. If a two-year-old doesn't like something in their mouth, they will insist on spitting it into your hand. I don't know what the science is here, but it's a fact, and the only alternative is for them to puke. Also, this will happen while you're driving on the freeway and they are strapped into the car seat. Do your stretches.

35. Two-year-olds can take their diapers off. This is not a drill. Buy disinfecting spray. Lots of it.

36. They will never wear themselves out. They just won't. Two-year-olds are the reality of perpetual motion. Two-year-olds are your cardio.

37. If you put a two-year-old to bed two hours late, they will get up two hours earlier. It's science.

38. If you get a dog, realize that your two-year-old will try to stick their fingers, toys, and food in it. You do the math.

39. Spray 'n Wash (by the case).

40. Caffeine.

Sure, there are more pro tips; there always are. But this should get you started. Stay safe, friends. Stay sane . . .

Sometimes They Really Nail the Gift-Giving Thing

When I opened my Father's Day gift to find a "Best Dad Ever" T-shirt with the bloated Daddy Pig (Peppa Pig's father) on it, I groaned. I didn't know if my two-year-old Aspen actually picked this gift out, but I'm 90 percent sure she had a hand in it. There were a number of clues. She's the only *Peppa Pig* fan. It also looked like it'd been wrapped by an asylum patient with wadded *Mickey Mouse Clubhouse* Christmas wrapping paper, half of it twisted inside out, and close to an entire roll of masking tape holding it together. There were a few crayon scribbles on the paper. I'd say they were in Aspen's handwriting, but she couldn't really write yet. I will admit, though, I knew her pen strokes well. They were on most of our furniture, the refrigerator, and several walls. But the real giveaway was how she reacted when I opened the gift.

She screamed, "Daddy Pig!" Then she tore it from my hands, mouth open, and hugged it. I didn't get the shirt back until later that night, after she'd gone to bed. She fell asleep with it wrapped in her arms.

I don't know if I've ever gotten a gift from my children I actually wanted. And I know that makes me sound like a crappy gift receiver. Is there a better word for that? Perhaps it just makes me a jerk, but I don't like to say that. I don't like calling myself a jerk because my kids give crappy gifts that were purchased as gifts for me but were obviously just for themselves. For example: One year for Father's Day, Tristan gave me a poop emoji pillow. He laughed and laughed over that sucker. It's now in his bed. Once, for my birthday, Norah gave me a bag of peanut butter cups, her favorite candy. I asked for one, and she told me no. I took one anyway, and she acted all butt-hurt about it and called me a mean daddy for taking some of my own Father's Day candy. I've gotten *Pokémon* cards, video games, Disney Princess DVDs (and not the good movies, the low-budget secondary films where all the princesses have a tea party), *PAW Patrol* coloring books . . . I could go on, but you get the idea. My kids aren't all that good at giving gifts. They kind of suck at it, actually. They think a little more about themselves when shopping. But I suppose it's their job to suck at giving gifts, and it's my job to help them figure out how to do it right. Particularly before they get married.

Not that I'm all that good at giving gifts (full confession). I usually just send cash in an envelope, no card, which basically places me somewhere between an uncle and a drug dealer. Long story short, there's no hope for any of us.

But you know what? The craziest thing happened with that Daddy Pig T-shirt. I refused to wear it for a long time. The moment I opened the gift and saw what it was, I made an oath to never wear it. I went weeks. It just sat there, in my closet, announcing my "Best Dad Ever" status to no one. It was Mel who brought it up, actually. We were in our bedroom, and she pulled the shirt out of the closet, and said, "Have you worn this?"

Not that I'm all that good at giving gifts (full confession). I usually just send cash in an envelope, no card, which basically places me somewhere between an uncle and a drug dealer. Long story short, there's no hope for any of us.

I shrugged and said something to the tune of who the gift was *really* for, and how I didn't want to look like a nerd, and how I wasn't that big of a *Peppa Pig* fan in the first place. Mel held it up to my chest and asked me to put it on for the day. Then she winked like she knew something I didn't, which she does pretty regularly, and it always drives me crazy.

I gave her an epic eye roll.

Then I relented and slid that sucker over my body.

It's a Saturday, I thought. *I could change before I go out, if needed.* I stepped into the living room slowly, reluctantly, feeling like Ralphie wearing that pink bunny suit in *A Christmas Story*.

Aspen was slashing at a coloring book on the living room floor, stomach on the ground, legs kicking, crayon in her fist like it was a knife. She didn't even look up at me until Mel asked her to. But then something happened. She smiled. She giggled. She jumped to her feet, and she hugged me. Then she put her hand on my chest, touched Daddy Pig, and laughed.

Now here's the thing: I'm a dad. And as a father, I will always be second fiddle to my wife. If both of us were in the room and Aspen got hurt, she'd go to Mom. I could literally stand between her and Mel, and she'd beeline around me, tears in her eyes, and go to her mother. If I'd try to stop her physically, she'd try to bite me. Mom always gets the best hugs, and snuggles, and kisses. Always. And I know that this is a source of tension for both Mel and me. Sometimes she feels suffocated by all this attention, while I'm often jealous of it. I wouldn't mind being the number one parent in the room every once in a while.

Now the last thing I'm saying is that my Daddy Pig shirt made my daughter love me more than her mother. I mean, I wouldn't say that out loud. At least not while Mel was in the room. But I will admit, it at least tipped the scales a little bit— just enough that I got a good 20 percent snuggle increase, and as a father, that felt like double the love I received from my daughter.

After that moment, I started wearing the Daddy Pig shirt every weekend. I never wore it to work because I work in a Division I athletics program. I'd probably get beat up. But any time I knew I was going to be around Aspen, I wore it. And every time I wore the shirt, she hugged me. She snuggled her head into my chest and said, "Daddy Pig." Or she screamed, ran to me, and tugged at my shirt so I'd bend down and pick her up. Or she'd let out this deep, contagious laugh that filled my chest with this rich, warm feeling that I'd never felt until I was a father.

The way she insisted on holding me made it the most fashionable thing I owned. It made that shirt the best gift I've ever received. I looked like a four-alarm nerdy father walking around the grocery store in that thing, but with Aspen snuggling me, none of that mattered.

The Threenager

Disneyland Is Awesome Unless You Take a Potty-Training Three-Year-Old

We'd been in line to meet Minnie Mouse for almost thirty minutes when Aspen reached up, tugged at my shorts, pulled up her Minnie Mouse dress, and pointed at the dark wet spot on her Minnie Mouse underwear. Pee dripped down her legs and into her Minnie Mouse socks and matching light-up shoes.

Mel was on her toes, trying to find the end of the line, which seemed to drift on into the eternities, winding through Minnie's purple and pink plastic house and well off behind us into Mickey's Toontown. I tapped Mel's shoulder and pointed. She looked down at our daughter, who was still holding up her dress. Then she looked at me and said, "Seriously?"

Tristan and Norah were somewhere else in the park with Mel's parents because no one wanted to meet Minnie Mouse except Aspen. Not Tristan or Norah. Not Mel. Definitely not I, yet there we were, standing in an hour-plus line, waiting to meet some poor college-age individual dressed in a massive mouse costume with exaggerated hands and feet.

Aspen laughed. Then she put her hands on her hips, looked up at her mother, and said, "Seriously?" in a snarky tone that made me want to abandon her at the park. I thought a lot about abandoning her on that trip, and most of it had to do with her peeing her pants.

She was supposed to be potty trained.

But what does that even mean? I wanted to believe she was. That's the thing with potty training—it doesn't exactly have a sharp ending, per se. There's not a final turning point, or test, or blessing, when you can say, "Yes! Now it's done. Let's enjoy our pee-free life." It's more of a drawn-out, gradual thing, like a Netflix series that may go on for two seasons or ten seasons—the creators don't really know because it's all based on views, so they just keep giving short moments of resolution at the end of each season along with a cliff-hanger, without ever answering the pressing question: "When will it all end?"

I simply didn't know, but I must admit, I was stupid enough to assume it had ended when we booked this trip, as if I hadn't potty trained two other children.

And to say Aspen was excited to meet Minnie Mouse was an understatement. It was all she talked about all day in her broken toddler English.

It felt like the whole park was in line to meet Minnie. It was the first two weeks of December. The Christmas lights were up, but most kids weren't out of school yet, so it wasn't too busy. But this was the longest line we'd been in. And to say Aspen was excited to meet Minnie Mouse was an understatement. It was all she talked about all day in her broken toddler English.

"We meet a Minnie?"

"She's not there yet. Later today."

"We meet a Minnie?"

"Later today."

"We meet a Minnie, *now*!"

The stakes were high.

The kid desperately wanted to meet this mouse.

The line snaked in and out and around, and we were well in it when Aspen peed her pants. There was only a short window of time to meet Minnie. It's not like she was there all day. The parents behind us had some crazy eyes, the kind you get only while waiting in line with a toddler to meet a mouse at Disneyland. One of us could easily get out with Aspen, but getting back in line could get us killed.

We were faced with a decision: step out and lose our spot (having wasted who knows how much time in line), risk a meltdown, and miss Minnie altogether; or change our daughter right there, in front of God and everyone, like a bunch of hillbillies.

Not that we hadn't already looked like hillbillies on this vacation. This was day two of a three-day trip. We were staying in the Disneyland Hotel. It was supposed to be our big, awesome family vacation, but it had mostly been Mel and I handling a soggy three-year-old.

On the first day she peed her pants waiting in line to get into the park. Then again on the Dumbo ride, and again on It's a Small World.

We ran out of clean underwear when the cannons on the Pirates of the Caribbean startled her.

That morning, before we left for the park, on the magical fiber-optic, light-up musical headboard, and the bathroom counter, and the windowsill, and the dresser, were pairs of Aspen's underwear that I'd washed in the bathroom sink with hand soap and set out to dry the night before. On the first day she peed her pants waiting in line to get into the park. Then again on the Dumbo ride, and again on It's a Small World.

We ran out of clean underwear when the cannons on the Pirates of the Caribbean startled her. Each time I took her to the potty, she wouldn't need to go because she'd already gone in her pants, and the second we got in line or on a ride— *boom*—waterworks.

The Disneyland Hotel was one of the nicest hotels we'd ever stayed at as a family. Draping our room in handwashed toddler underwear felt pretty trashy.

But there were a few reasons for doing this.

We flew into the park then took a shuttle to the hotel, so we couldn't exactly drive anywhere to buy new underwear. I looked into using a washing machine at the hotel, but they didn't have them, only a laundry service—and when I checked the price and thought about how this vacation felt like it cost as much as a trip to the moon, I didn't exactly feel comfortable paying the cost of an additional airline ticket to get my daughter's underwear cleaned. I looked into buying more underwear at the park but could find only churros and turkey legs, both of which I'm convinced contained nicotine because they were so habit forming.

And naturally, we had some diapers that we

planned to use for nighttime, but using those during the day . . . Well, it felt like failure. It felt like taking a step backward. More than anything, putting our daughter back in diapers, even for just a few days, felt like all that hard work we'd put in over the summer to get this kid potty trained was for nothing and she'd probably spend an eternity peeing her pants. And eventually, around age thirty-five, she'd be on a daytime talk show, confessing that the reason she blew up a federal building was because her parents didn't teach her to pee in the toilet.

Was that too far?

Maybe.

But unless you've potty trained a toddler, you have no idea what it's like.

Before our trip to Disneyland, Mel had the summer off from her teaching job, so it was now or never to potty train Aspen before going back to daycare.

So we basically lived in a urine-soaked hell for two months in which all wet spots were suspicious and nothing brown on the floor was ever chocolate.

And I know there are some parents who preach about just waiting until the child figures it out, but with both of us working full time, we didn't have that option. So we basically lived in a urine-soaked hell for two months in which all wet spots were suspicious and nothing brown on the floor was ever chocolate.

For those of you who haven't yet endured the nightmare of potty training, here's a preview . . .

It looked like Mel running down the hallway with a toddler in her outstretched arms, the child crying and leaking fluid down her legs, while Mel cried, "In the potty! It goes in the potty!"

It looked like a short blonde child hiding in a closet to poop in her underwear then walking around the house with an egg-size bulge in the back of her pants, the whole time denying that she'd obviously pooped her pants.

It looked like a half-naked toddler sitting on the toilet like *The Thinker* sculpture, her face full of concentration to get the job done, and me feeling a short swell of pride that maybe, just maybe, she was figuring this whole potty thing out and I could finally shampoo the carpet.

It looked like me accidentally asking a coworker, "Is it time to use the potty?" because it had become such a refrain.

It looked like celebrating her first time pooping in the toilet as though it were an acceptance letter from Harvard Medical School.

It looked like waking up in the early morning to hear her open the restroom door, climb onto the toilet, and do her business on her own, while I listened to her tinkle as though it were the most satisfying sound in the history of humanity.

Potty training isn't for the weak. Yet, there we were at Disneyland, and all she could do was pee her pants over and over again.

And sure, it wasn't her fault.

Technically.

Suddenly my wife and I were changing our daughter's underwear in the middle of the Magic Kingdom, a line of people behind us and a line of people ahead of us, trying to act all casual about it.

Disneyland is an exciting place with a million distractions. But my goodness, she was striking out at this park. We'd been there for almost thirty hours, and she hadn't had a successful trip to the potty yet, and all of it was incredibly frustrating and made me feel like all the hard work we'd put into teaching this kid to do something as basic as pee in the toilet had gone out the window. Suddenly my wife and I were changing our daughter's underwear in the middle of the Magic Kingdom, a line of people behind us and a line of people ahead of us, trying to act all casual about it.

But we did it, and we almost felt good about it . . . until it happened again, five people from Minnie.

This time Aspen told Mel.

"Seriously?" I said.

Aspen shrugged. Mel told me we were out of

underwear. All of it, every piece I'd washed the night before had been peed in.

I looked down at my daughter. I pointed at her. I was that parent, giving my three-year-old a lecture in line at Disneyland. I told her to knock it off. I asked her to try harder. I said things like, "This is ridiculous," and, "You had this down," and, "You need to stop."

Then I said something that seemed to hit home with the child, ultimately turning the tide and making me feel like dad garbage.

"Are you even trying?" I said with my fists clenched at my sides.

She held this straight hangdog look, eyes just a little misty. She stopped looking at me and started looking at the ground.

Mel and I discussed the situation. We wondered if it was wrong to put a wet toddler on Minnie Mouse's lap. Were we horrible to think of doing it? Had it happened before? Were we not the first people to do it?

I didn't know the answers to any of these questions. But what I can say is that I was frustrated. I was embarrassed. I felt hopeless. I wondered if my daughter ever would pee in the toilet like a regular human.

By the time I stopped pondering, we were next to the mouse, who was sitting in some big, red, plastic, cartoonlike chair, wearing a red and white polka-dot dress and exaggerated pointy yellow shoes. Before I had a chance to say anything, Mel picked up our squishy little girl and placed her on Minnie's lap.

Perhaps it was because it was so close to Christmas, or maybe it was the lights that were already beginning to come on around the park, but Aspen started asking Minnie for things as though she were Santa: a *Peppa Pig* play set, a *PAW Patrol* book, a Minnie Mouse costume . . . She went on for quite a while, Minnie's massive head nodding the whole time, her big white gloves around Aspen's waist.

It seemed obvious that Minnie's helpers, two female college interns, were about to ask us to take Aspen off Minnie's lap, when Aspen said, "And to use the potty."

I froze when she said that. Then she looked at Mel and me, and she leaned in closer to Minnie and softly said, "Really good. To use the potty really good."

I didn't know what to say. There was part of me—the part that had been fighting with that kid for hours, days, and months to use the potty— that assumed she hated to use the potty. But she obviously had a desire to use it and that made me realize she was trying. And although I felt like a potty-training failure up until that moment, it all turned on a dime and I realized something had gotten through to her.

Mel pulled Aspen off Minnie's lap. Then, once

we were away from the line, next to that music-making fountain in the heart of Toontown, I crouched down and said, "I know you've had some accidents at the park today. But I know you've been trying, and I'm proud of you. I'm sorry for getting mad."

She didn't smile. She didn't look away. She didn't laugh or yell. She just put her arms around my neck and gave me a hug. We stayed like that until my knees hurt from crouching.

I went to stand up, but she said, "Hold'a me."

"But you peed your pants," I said.

She repeated it, "Hold'a me."

I reluctantly picked her up, and placed her on my hip, feeling the still-warm pee soak through my new Space Mountain T-shirt. Then we headed back to the hotel to handwash underwear.

If You Haven't Carried Your Child Out of a Store Like a Kicking and Screaming Surfboard, Have You Even Parented Today?

We stopped at Barnes & Noble on our way to the swimming pool so my seven-year-old, Norah, could pick out a book with her birthday money. My three-year-old, Aspen, found a *Peppa Pig* backpack on the shelf and cradled it in her arms like it was her firstborn.

She was in a *Peppa Pig* swimming suit and *Peppa Pig* socks and shoes. Everything right then was about that stupid, poorly drawn British pig.

Each night for the past three months, I read the same story about Peppa getting on her grandfather's train and looking for bridges and trees, which they always found—but they never seemed to find my sanity. And each night I thought about hiding that stupid book in the garbage can; but I didn't, because I knew if I did, she wouldn't go to sleep the next night without reading about Grandpa Pig's train. But everything with Aspen was like that. She was always one step ahead, knowing just how to push my buttons. And in that bookstore, I knew I was between a rock and a hard place.

But here's the real kicker: That *Peppa Pig* backpack, with the activity book and markers and little water bottle, well, we already had it. We bought it a few months ago at this same Barnes & Noble, in this same section. Sure, she wasn't in a swimming suit then. She was in shorts and a T-shirt, also with Peppa Pig on it, but none of that matters, because she pulled the same move. She hugged, and cried, and wouldn't let it go, so I bought it for her because it was on sale and it seemed educational. Plus, I was planning to buy her something at the store anyway, so it didn't seem like that big of a deal.

But had I created a monster by giving in to her that one time? Did this mean she'd never leave my house because she'd now lost all sense of work ethic and independence and would be dependent on Mel and I her whole life, living in our basement like some overweight, pasty marshmallow of a human? Or worse, would she grow up to become some sort of obsessive cartoon-pig lover, throwing fits in bookstores while dressed as a pig in hopes of generating a massive YouTube following?

As a father, I often felt like I was supposed to assume that any time I gave in to my toddler I was ruining them.

Was I overreacting?

Gosh, I don't know.

Maybe.

It was hard to think that far ahead. Yet, as a father, I often felt like I was supposed to assume that any time I gave in to my toddler I was ruining them.

Or at least that's what one out of every five online commenters on my blog led me to believe.

She was pulling the same moves she did the last time I bought it for her, and I think she assumed I'd do it again. She chanted "Peppa" over and over while holding the stupid thing to her chest, swaying side to side, her face soft and sweet. It was the face kids are born with that makes a parent melt.

I explained to her that she already had the same bag at home, but there was no reasoning with her. She was three. Reasoning with a three-year-old felt like reasoning with a goat.

In her little mind, she wanted *all* the things. I once had to pry a box of condoms out of her hands because it happened to be open and she thought they were balloons. No amount of reasoning with her could've calmed her down. It was embarrassing all around, particularly when one of the store clerks asked if everything was okay, and I said, "I'm just telling my daughter she can't buy . . ." I paused for a moment, then pointed at the open box of condoms. "Those." The clerk, a man in his early twenties and probably childless, gave me a sideways glance that seemed to say, "You wouldn't be here if you'd used one of those."

I wanted to punch him in the face, but I was busy with a fit-throwing three-year-old, so I let it go. I think a lot of nonparents' lives are saved because the parent they just insulted with their snide glance is too busy managing their toddler to kick their trash.

Anyway, in that moment at the bookstore, I was faced with two decisions as a father: I could buy her a toy she already had, which was impractical but would save her melting down at the store. Or I could take the bag from her and risk an epic meltdown.

Aspen had a couple of choices too. She could listen to her father and put the thing back. That would be the adult thing to do. But she was three, and teaching her to make those kinds of decisions was my job.

It was her job to be a turd about it.

As a father of toddlers, I've been faced with this decision countless times. And sometimes I give in, like I did when we were at this same bookstore and I bought her the dumb bag the first time. And sometimes it just doesn't make sense, so I dig in my heels and face the inevitable public meltdown.

She was three, and teaching her
to make those kinds of decisions
was my job.

It was her job to be a turd about it.

I waited until Mel and Noiah were finished shopping, and then I pried the toy out of Aspen's arms as she screamed like I'd actually removed a limb and I tried not to hurt her, the whole time wondering if she was actually an Avenger because of her freakishly strong grip.

I hauled Aspen out of the store underneath my arm, her screaming in a *Peppa Pig* swimming suit, legs kicking, my swimming suit falling down, half my crack showing, my hands unable to pull my swimming suit up because they were full. Everyone at the bookstore looked at us. They peeked up from behind their paperbacks and newspapers. They stopped their conversations in the coffee shop. They paused their transactions at the register. It was like a bomb went off, a three-year-old toddler bomb (which isn't as bad as a nuclear bomb, but at close range feels just as deadly).

Am I being too dramatic?

I can answer this one myself: No.

> If I ever apply for a job and during the interview they ask if I can handle working in a high-stress environment, I will bring up this moment, and they will nod and hand me the job.

No, I'm not, because dragging a screaming child out of a bookstore is a horrible feeling, and I hope to never do it again. If I ever apply for a job and during the interview they ask if I can handle working in a high-stress environment, I will bring up this moment, and they will nod and hand me the job. Right there. Probably with a raise and company car and unlimited cell phone data. No further questions, because I will have clearly proven my valor.

I got to the van, Aspen screaming and kicking the whole way to the parking lot. I was sweating a little and wondering if anyone was going to accuse me of kidnapping my own child, because frankly, it looked like a kidnapping. I got her buckled, which was pretty difficult with her trying to claw my face and kick my crotch. Then we sat in the van for some time, Mel and the two older kids still in line at the store, while I waited for Aspen to calm down.

Once it was all said and done, I looked at her in the back seat. Aspen was still a little red-faced, but she wasn't crying anymore (although her blonde hair was a sweaty fit mess and one of her shoes was missing).

Mel came to the van. She was wearing a pink and white striped camisole, her swimming suit beneath it, hair pulled into a tight braid. It was quiet. My forehead was resting on the steering wheel, hands on my knees.

"Well, that was intense," she said. "What happened?"

Until I had children, I never realized how emotionally draining it is on a parent, nor did I realize that no matter what a parent does in a situation like this, there really is no way to win.

I explained. Then I said, "For a hot minute I thought about buying it for her. You know, just giving in because it would be easier than what I'm feeling right now."

"What are you feeling right now?" she asked.

I thought for a moment. "Rage. Frustration."

I paused. "But mostly embarrassment."

She rubbed my back but quickly stopped and commented, "You're also a little sweaty."

"Did I do the right thing?" I asked.

Before becoming a parent, I must have seen this scene played out a million and one times in a bazillion stores. But until I had children, I never realized how emotionally draining it is on a parent, nor did I realize that no matter what a parent does in a situation like this, there really is no way to win. I was either going to create an expectation that if my child grabs something at the store, I will buy it for them regardless. Or I will end up disrupting everyone in a twenty-mile radius as I work to establish boundaries with my child.

Mel thought for a moment. Then she said, "You reinforced a boundary. You disrupted a quiet bookstore to do it, and you got a little embarrassed. But I know you did what was best for Aspen. It sucked. But you did it. I'm proud of you."

I looked in the rearview mirror. Aspen was asleep now. Tristan and Norah were buckled in, eager to get to the pool.

I took a breath.

"Well, I'm glad someone is," I said.

Mel placed Aspen's missing *Peppa Pig* shoe on the dashboard.

"A woman handed it to me as I left the store. I don't know how she knew we were together, but she wanted me to tell you something."

"What's that?" I asked.

"That my husband was a good man."

I gave her a half-smile, laughed a little, and we headed to the pool.

It's Cool—
Sometimes you
Just Have to
Bribe the Kid

Yeah, I get it. People have been telling parents since the dawn of parenting not to bribe their children because it turns them into future jerks who expect something for nothing. At least, that's what my mother says. She says that's what is wrong with my generation. You know, the generation she helped raise.

But here's the reality: We all bribe our kids. Every single one of us. So, like always, I'm here to set the record straight. I'm going to have the conversation no one else feels comfortable having.

Following are just a few of the many situations when it's totally okay to bribe your toddler. You're welcome.

- When your toddler puts up a screaming fit about getting ready for bed at the end of a fourteen-hour workday and all you want is for them to get dressed for bed because the day won't end until their little smelly butt is in bed, but they're fighting and it makes you want to box your own ears to kill the sound, it's okay to bribe them with M&M's to get things moving.

- When you're at the store and your toddler keeps screaming because they want to push the cart, so you let them, and they end up smashing into a display of pickles, busting several bottles and making a smelly mess in the pickle section, so you put the kid in the cart so they won't get cut with broken glass, but the child won't stop screaming because they want to push the stupid cart again, which you know is a bad decision, it's okay to bribe them with a free cookie from the bakery.

- When your toddler gets up somewhere between 3:00 a.m. and 4:00 a.m. and refuses to go back to sleep regardless of how many times you ask them to sleep in your bed or give them ultimatums or explain to them rationally that you have a lot going on tomorrow and you really need your sleep (as if they actually care about you and your life in the slightest), it's okay to break the screen-time limit and let them watch *Bubble Guppies* for the next several hours in their bed so you can get the sleep you need to keep from getting fired.

- When your toddler looks at the healthy lemon salmon and broccoli you slaved over as though it were sewage mixed with fish guts and they gag and get all red-faced and start crying each time you attempt to put it in their mouth, while your food is getting cold and it's making *you* want to cry because this happens to be your favorite meal, it's okay to bribe them with ice cream to shut up and eat a few small bites.

- When you are on the freeway and your toddler is screaming and red-faced and pulling at their sibling's hair because the van seats are too close, and everything is chaos, it's okay to hand the child your cell phone so you don't roll the sucker and kill the whole family.

- When you're trying to leave the park so you can make it to a work meeting, but your toddler is dragging their feet and screaming and refusing to get buckled, and you don't have time for that crap because you are already late, it's okay to offer them a stick of gum from the glove box.

- When you're trying to get family pictures and the toddler keeps trying to take off their cute outfit, or won't stay out of the dirt, or won't stop putting their hands in their pants, and all you want is one picture to prove to the world that you're not actually raising a family of crazed feral swamp monsters, it's okay to promise a trip to the toy store if they smile really cute in one picture.

See? Sometimes it's totally justifiable to bribe your kids. Heck, if you look at the driving-on-the-freeway example, a bribe might just save your whole family. Don't stress too much about it. There's no need. I have a strong feeling that none of this will show up on their college application. It's not going to keep them out of Oxford, and it's not going to send them to jail. But it will help you keep one thread of sanity—and sometimes that's all you have left.

Threenagers Talk a Lot of Smack for Someone with Crocs on the Wrong Feet

---

My toddlers have talked some smack. Sometimes it feels like they learned "yes," "no," "hot," "cold," and smack talk. And it's not like they have the right to talk smack. I mean, honestly, what have they accomplished? Toddlers can't drive a car or keep track of their shoes.

I know some of you are like, "If a toddler talks smack but they don't understand that they are being rude, does it still count as smack?" Well, that's a tough question. It feels like asking about a tree falling in the woods with no one around. What you're really asking is, "Should parents take toddler smack personally?" I try not to. I try to laugh it off. But sometimes it doesn't work. Sometimes it cuts

213

too close to the core, and I cannot help but look at my little smack talker and give them some of my own smack talk.

Not that any of that works.

Toddlers don't listen.

Anyway, here are a few examples of what I'm talking about (names of toddlers have been removed to protect the sweet, innocent children who talk smack):

- Three-year-old pushing on my thirty-something gut: "Daddy, are you going to have a baby?"

- Sick in bed with a cold: "Daddy, old people die."

- Grabbing their mother's butt: "This is squishy . . . too squishy."

- "What are you cooking? It smells like the dog."

- "Please bless that Dad will stop being so bad at *Mario Kart*. Amen."

- "Dad! Slow down! You drive like a bad guy!"

- "The beans smell like Dad's morning mouth."

- Wife burps: "Stop mouth farting!"

Silence Is a Scary Sound

- Me: "I love you."
  Three-year-old: "I love Mom."

- "You are the meanest person on Mean Island!"

- "Daddy, your singing is making me sad."

- I ask for a hug at daycare drop-off: "Daddy! Can you please leave?"

- "You're never going to be my best friend!"

- I sprain my ankle at the park.
  Three-year-old: "Push me on the swing!"
  Me: "I can't walk right now."
  Three-year-old: "You could crawl."

- "I was good today. What's my treat?"
  "You can have some of my hugs and kisses."
  "I don't like any of those."

- Picking them up at daycare.
  Me: "How was your day?"
  Three-year-old: "I was on fire today!"
  Me: "Is that a good thing?"
  Three-year-old: (*Nods excitedly.*)
  Daycare worker: (*Mouths, "No."*)

- "Daddy! Your job is to kill the bugs, and if you can't . . ." (*Ominously gestures to the door.*)

- "Give me your phone or I'll fart in your mouth!"

- We pass a man with an eye patch at the mall.
  Three-year-old: (*Whispers something.*)
  Me: "What?"
  Three-year-old (*loudly*): "That guy's a pirate!"

- "Mommy, your legs look like our lawn."

- "You ruined my whole entire life!"

- "Daddy, I love you. But mostly I love your iPad."

- "It's only okay to cheat when I do it!"

- Three-year-old comes home from daycare: "We don't need'a be friends anymore now that I have real friends."

Do you see what I'm talking about? I could go on. I have so many. But I think I got my point across. Threenager: the original gangster. But take comfort in knowing that eventually your child develops a filter. But then the question becomes, Do they just say the same things, maybe worse, in their heads? Who knows. But if I were a betting man, I'd say yes.

You Aren't Going to Get Anything Done, So You Might as Well Build a Fort

I was home from work on a Friday. Mel was teaching, and Tristan and Norah were at school. I gave Aspen the iPad so I could fold two baskets of laundry without her bothering me. Instead, she climbed on my leg while watching *Max and Ruby* and wanted me to tug her around the house.

She looked up at me with these bright wonderful eyes, like this was the best thing that had ever happened, and I looked down at her and asked her to stop and kicked my leg a bit, trying to shake her off. But her grip was just too strong and I couldn't break it, so I ended up dragging her around the house like a ball and chain, the laundry basket in my hands, cursing and wishing she'd give me just a few moments to get the laundry put away.

It took almost twenty minutes to get her off of me, and during that time I might have put away three shirts.

I sat her down at the table with some vanilla wafers, thinking that would distract her so I could get the rest of the laundry put away. I was stupid enough to leave her with the box of wafers—she poured them all out on the table and took a nickel-size bite out of each one. There were easily forty wafers in that box.

Why did she do this?

Because three-year-olds are anarchists.

My work schedule at the university was a little wonky at this time. During the summers I worked five days a week, but during the school year, I worked two evenings and took Fridays off. Every Friday, Aspen was a terror. But this was my first Friday off after the summer, and somehow in that time my memory had become soft and I'd forgotten how horrible it was to try to do anything with her around.

I cleaned up the wafers, and she threw a fit. A big, nasty, boogery fit, where she screamed at me for taking away her "cookies." So I gave her a few of the wafers she'd taken a bite out of, but she didn't want those cookies because they'd already been eaten.

"No," I said, "they are still good. You took one bite. You can still eat them."

But she didn't like that response. She wanted

me to get a new box of wafers, which I didn't have, but she also didn't want me to clean up the wafers that were on the table because they were hers. All of it was such a twisted leap of logic that I wanted to blow up a Nabisco factory—but I didn't have time for that sort of thing because I couldn't even get my laundry put away.

Then she peed in her swimming suit,
so I rushed her to the restroom, and
as I put her swimming suit in the laundry,
she shoved a dishrag in the toilet
and flooded the bathroom.

Once I got that situation handled, fit and all, Aspen insisted on pouring her own milk. Naturally, I had another mess to deal with. Then she wanted to change into her *Peppa Pig* swimming suit even though I had no intentions of letting her swim.

Then she peed in her swimming suit, so I rushed her to the restroom, and as I put her swimming suit in the laundry, she shoved a dishrag in the toilet and flooded the bathroom.

I swore. I swore a lot . . .

Then she had the nerve to ask me to put her into another swimming suit, which I did because I was obviously her bitch.

All said and done, it took me almost two hours to put two baskets of clean laundry away.

Two hours. My frustration level was eleven, and

I ended up sitting on the table, eating the vanilla wafers Aspen didn't finish.

> All said and done, it took me almost two hours to put two baskets of clean laundry away.

Mel and I both worked, so we took a lot of turns with the kids, almost like two wrestlers tagging in then tagging out. But one thing was consistent: With a three-year-old in the house, nothing really got done. Our home was in a constant state of distress. There were always dishes in the sink, and the moment they got put away, the laundry would pile up, and the moment that was taken care of, the three-year-old spilled her crackers or wanted some cheese or decided to color the walls. Every day with Aspen at this stage felt like chasing a guerilla terrorist group.

The moment I assumed we'd squashed it out, she'd organize another anarchist demonstration somewhere else in the house.

Around lunchtime, I was ready to lose my mind when Mel called home to check on me.

"How's it going?" she asked.

I vented. I told her about the toilet and the wafers and the swimming suit and how long it took me to put away two loads of laundry. The whole time she was silent. I couldn't see her face, but I had confidence that her eyes were rolling. She had the summer off, so she'd just finished spending all summer at home with our little terrorist.

Once I was done, I expected her to laugh at me. I expected her to say something to the tune of, "Stop complaining. I did it all summer, every day—you are just dealing with her on Friday."

Every day with Aspen at this stage felt like chasing a guerilla terrorist group.

But she didn't. All she said was, "Do something fun with her."

I paused for a moment, not sure what to say.

"How can I do that when the house is a wreck?" I said.

"Stop what you are doing, and do something fun," she said. "What's more important right now? Cleaning the house? Or spending time with your daughter? You got some stuff done, now have fun with her. It'll be okay."

I thought about what she was saying. I mean, I didn't think long because it was suddenly quiet in the house, and I've already discussed what that means (see page 59). But I thought long enough to reflect on all the times I'd called home during the summer and Mel had vented to me about how she wasn't getting anything done. I never told her to do something fun. I'd make suggestions, brilliant suggestions, as a way to help her fix the problem. And she'd always let out a long sigh, which I assumed meant she thought I was right—but it turned out it was more about my not getting it.

"Is this what you always wanted me to say when I called home over the summer?"

"Yup," she replied.

"I just can't give up, though," I said. "There's too much to do."

"You will, though," she said. "You can't win with a three-year-old."

I kept trying to get the laundry done, but Aspen wanted a sandwich. A sandwich she refused to eat, so I ate it. I tried to do the dishes, but she climbed in the dishwasher. I tried to clean off the table while talking to my mother, but Aspen tried to eat the dog's food.

I had big plans at the beginning of the day to get the house in shape, and Aspen undermined them all, so midafternoon I took Mel's advice, and we built a fort.

> I kept trying to get the laundry done, but Aspen wanted a sandwich. A sandwich she refused to eat, so I ate it.

Not that I wanted to build a fort. I didn't. I haven't wanted to build a fort in the living room since I was a little boy. But Aspen did and I'd given up fighting.

We put a large blanket over the couch and the

easy chair. We added a dining room chair and a few pillows. We had a front and back door. Aspen fit comfortably inside the fort, while my legs awkwardly hung out the back end.

We sat in the thing and started laughing. We played with puzzles. I tickled her, and she tickled me. And before I knew it, Mel came home to us giggling in the living room, the house still a mess.

Mel poked her head inside and said, "Having fun?"

Tristan and Norah had come home with Mel, and they climbed in with us. Not that there was necessarily enough room, but they made it work by climbing on top of me.

We all had an awesome time in that fort despite the dishes still in the sink, and the dirty laundry, and the unmade beds. I don't know if Aspen will remember all this, but I know I will. There was a warmth in that fort that will stick with me forever—and when I think about that, I realize that sometimes building a fort is more important than, well, anything.

Stupid Questions I've Been Asked While Caring for a Threenager and the Answers I'd Love to Give

———————————

Having a toddler made me moody, and when nonparents asked me questions about my toddler (which happened regularly), I got kind of, well . . . I wanted to karate chop them in the throat. Would that have sent me to jail? Probably. The rational side, the adult side, the side that could see beyond the fits, understood that I couldn't go before a judge and say, "I karate chopped that man because he asked me a stupid question about my toddler." It just wouldn't hold up in court. So I had to pause and realize that they were well-intentioned questions.

I always answered graciously.

But inside, I just couldn't.

Here are a few examples.

- "How do you keep up with that little guy?" What were you expecting from this question? That I'd break down in tears and admit that I can't keep up with my three-year-old? Well, yeah. I can't. Sometimes I can't catch him because he's freaking fast. But then there's the metaphorical end of keeping up with his messes and wanting and needing and pooping. Sometimes I just want to pull an *Eat Pray Love* and run off to Europe and find myself again. But I can't afford that. And I'd probably miss my kid . . . eventually. Sorry. I'm rambling. I'm tired. How do I manage him? Not very well. Is that the answer you were looking for? Are you satisfied? Now I'm crying.

- "What's that white stuff on your shirt?" Boogers. It's always boogers. Tomorrow there will be boogers on my clothes again. If the stain is something other than white, it's pee or poop. Deal with it.

- "Did you see last night's episode of *This Is Us*?" (This doesn't seem to be a question about a three-year-old, but it is.) I don't control the TV anymore. The three-year-old does. Last night

I watched *Yo Gabba Gabba!* Then I watched eight hundred million renditions of "The Finger Family Song" on YouTube. Then I thought about cutting my eyes out of my skull. Check it out: If the protagonist isn't animated, or isn't stuffed, or isn't some kid opening a magic egg, or doesn't have their hand up a puppet's butthole, just assume I haven't seen it.

- "Are they worth it?" You know, it wasn't a good investment. I'm still upside down on this kid. In the red. Billions and billions. And he's not exactly bringing much in. Or anything. So no, I'd say it was a bad investment. However, I should add that the last time I was pooping, my three-year-old barged in and offered me Froot Loops, so the snacks are pretty good.

- "Are you getting enough sleep?" Are you friggin' serious? How much is enough? Enough to not commit homicide? Look me in the eyes. I'm right on the line. I was up for two hours last night changing wet sheets and searching for Bun-Bun. I want to put Bun-Bun in a garbage disposal . . .

- "Does your three-year-old ever talk back?" Oh, no way. She's a little angel. Most of the time she speaks in "pleases" and "thank-you's" and offers me tea in a rich British accent. Then

I put my feet up after a long day's work, and she brings me my slippers and makes me a sandwich. Of course she talks back! Yesterday she called me a penguin because I wouldn't let her watch Netflix. Then she called my wife a hobo because she wouldn't give her an ice cream sandwich. We didn't teach her to talk like that, but here we are.

- "Are you going to have another?" Look at me. I mean *really* look. I'm in Crocs and sweatpants. I haven't slept well in days, and I don't recall the last time I took a shower. I don't know who would actually sleep with me right now, and I'm so tired I'm not sure if I remember how. So yeah, it's not exactly on the schedule. Ask me once this one's in college.

- "I bet there is a lot of love in your home, right?" Mostly my home is full of poo, boogers, and wet spots that I don't understand. I can't explain all of the smells, and my table and chairs are sticky. But yes, when I come home, my three-year-old jumps into my arms, and it's wonderful. Then she shows me a new dance or something else adorable, and it always melts my heart.

Yes, there are more questions. So many more questions. But I suppose the moral of the story (if there is a moral) is: Don't ask questions when someone is living with a toddler. Wait. No, no, that's kind of mean. I think the moral is this: Toddlers can make you a little crazy and a lot irritable. Think of *Inside Out*. The red guy with fire for a head has the wheel. So if you see a toddler's parent struggling in the grocery store with a screaming three-year-old in the cart, just accept that they have their hands full. No further questions at this time.

"I'm Done! Wipe My Butt!"

I was home alone when my three-year-old went into the restroom to poop at the same time as the cat scratched at the front door. Aspen was in a pink and white *Peppa Pig* dress, a sock on one foot, her blonde hair tangled from making a blanket fort in the living room.

We'd been potty training, sure, and she'd gotten pretty good at the whole number two thing. She was like the John Madden of number two, announcing her movements in a play-by-play, beginning with "I poop" before strutting into the restroom. Once there, she cried, "I pooping" and she ended with, "I'm done! Wipe my butt!" Home, shopping, church, it didn't matter. She made sure everyone knew what was going on with number two. Number one, though? Well, that was negotiable. If I were to put a percentage on it, I'd say she was somewhere between 65 percent and 75 percent. Is that being too generous? I don't know, I studied English. What I do know is that every time she said she had to poop, I dreaded it. Why? Because although I was proud of her for making this leap toward independence, whenever I heard her say, "I'm done! Wipe my butt," I knew I had a 50 percent chance of being at the business end, cleaning some nastiness and wondering why I got into the parenting gig in the first place. I've been this way with all three of my children, and I don't care how rosy you try to paint parenting, wiping a three-year-old's butt is never satisfying. It's never rewarding. It just smells bad and makes me feel like a slave locked in butt-wiping servitude.

Aspen always cried, "I'm done! Wipe my butt!" into the heavens as if God, or some other great force, were going to reach from the clouds with a wipe and magically take care of her poopy butthole. But as much as I wanted Jesus to take the wheel, he never did. What really happened was Mel and I looked at each other for several seconds, like we have with *all* things poop related, waiting for the other to offer to handle the dreaded butt wiping.

"I did it last time."

"No, I did it last time."

"Don't lie."

"I'm not."

And so on . . .

However, we couldn't argue too long, because if we did Aspen would hop off the toilet, having done nothing with her poopy butt and making a huge skid across the toilet seat. Then she'd pull up her underwear, walk into the living room, and sit on the sofa, making the thing smell like poop for a week. Or she'd try to handle it herself, ultimately making what could only be described as poop expressionist art on the walls, toilet, and herself. Or she would eat it . . .

We couldn't argue too long, because if we did Aspen would hop off the toilet, having done nothing with her poopy butt and making a huge skid across the toilet seat. Then she'd pull up her underwear, walk into the living room, and sit on the sofa, making the thing smell like poop for a week.

The moment she yelled, "I'm done! Wipe my butt," we had roughly fifteen to twenty seconds before facing a mess of horrible proportions.

This time, however, as Aspen went to do her business, it was only me. I was the only one there to handle it. One hundred percent Dad.

The cat, Vincent, a black and white scrappy tuxedo cat that wandered the streets at night and often came back with cuts from fighting other cats, scratched at the door. He wanted to get in the garage for some food, but the dog was in the kitchen, and those two didn't get along.

Now here's the thing with the dog. His name was Pikachu after the *Pokémon* character. We let the kids name the dog, and originally they were trying to decide between Bob, Sparky, or Fart Squirrel. Somehow they landed on Pikachu, which, for me as a father, makes perfect sense because I hate *Pokémon* and I don't really care for dogs. Why wouldn't my children combine these two frustrations into one package in some subconscious effort to spite me?

Am I being too cynical here? It doesn't matter.

He was a small brown dog, with a long nose and pointy ears and short little dog legs. Dark eyes. A mutt. He was new to the family. We'd only gotten him a month or so earlier. During that time, we'd realized that he had some issues. He got carsick and threw up in the van. (Get *that* smell out, I dare you.) He got randy sometimes and made love to his dog bed, something I didn't understand considering he'd been neutered, but nevertheless I'd now had multiple conversations with my kids about the dog's boner and how it wouldn't hurt them. He chewed on stuff. He barked at the neighbors so much that they called the cops. But the one thing in particular I really couldn't live with was this: He was a rescue dog, which made me feel good when adopting him, but whoever owned him before must have been a man, and he must have abused him, because whenever I raised my voice or tried to pick him up, he rolled onto his back and peed in the air.

I kid you not.

Somehow they landed on Pikachu, which, for me as a father, makes perfect sense because I hate *Pokémon* and I don't really care for dogs. Why wouldn't my children combine these two frustrations into one package in some subconscious effort to spite me?

Me: "Kids! We're late! Get in the van." (*Dog rolls on his back and pees in the air.*)

Me: "Stop chewing on the sofa!" (*Dog rolls on his back and pees in the air.*)

Me: "Come on, Pikachu, let's go outside." (*I lean down to pick him up and take him outside and dog rolls on his back and pees in the air.*)

We probably should have named him Squirtle instead of Pikachu.

I had empathy for the dog, but the reality is that I felt like I was walking on eggshells with the little guy. And I'm sure there might be dog therapy, or dog medication, or something, but I didn't know where to begin with that, nor did I know how I'd afford it, and by the time I got new carpet I was going to need therapy myself.

I wanted to get rid of that dog so bad, yet every time I said, "This dog has to go," all three of my children crowded around Pikachu to form some sort of human shield. Not that I had any idea how to get rid of a dog. I mean, come on: What does that even look like? Would I take him back? Would I drop him off in the woods and drive away? Would I try to sell him on Craigslist? I wouldn't even know how to begin.

It was an empty threat.

But what I must say is that my older two kids, Tristan and Norah, didn't pull on my heartstrings quite like Aspen did when I wanted to get rid of Pikachu. It was her and her watery-eyed, tuck-lipped little face that made my heart melt. But ultimately, this is the power of a three-year-old.

If someone could harness the power of a three-year-old they'd rule the world. I have no doubt.

I don't know how they can make a parent's heart melt like that. I mean, I was constantly up in the night with the little lady for something as stupid as her sock coming off. She's peed on me, wiped boogers on me, puked on me, but her soft little face could make me do something crazy like keep a dog who peed in the air every time I raised my voice. Almost daily she had me wrist-deep in poop, wiping her butt. If someone could harness the power of a three-year-old they'd rule the world. I have no doubt.

"I'm pooping!" Aspen announced.

The cat was scratching the paint off the front door. I assumed I had time. I carried the cat across the living room of our small thousand-square-foot rural Oregon home and turned right at the kitchen, where the dog was sitting quietly.

I cradled Vincent in both hands, arms above my head, his paws dangling, his back arched.

Now listen, when we got the dog, I asked the pound to give me their finest dog, but I was never told exactly what kind of dog he was. Looking at him, I'm pretty sure he was a mix of dachshund and Chihuahua. But it turns out one of those breeds can jump incredibly high. I'm not a tall man. I stand about five feet six. I probably should live in a tree and make fudge, so I suppose I couldn't have held Vincent all that high, just above my head. Pikachu leaped in the air and came inches from biting the cat. I held the cat higher, with one hand. He hissed and clawed and bit my right arm.

And suddenly I was left with a decision as to what to handle first: the mess on the kitchen floor, my poopy toddler, or my bleeding and peed-on self.

I yelled, "Knock it off, Pikachu!"

He looked up at me, something twisted behind his dark eyes, and then he sprawled out on his back and showered pee on the carpet, the kitchen linoleum, and the side of my leg.

It was then that Aspen cried, "I'm done! Wipe my butt!"

And suddenly I was left with a decision as to what to handle first: the mess on the kitchen floor, my poopy toddler, or my bleeding and peed-on self. As a father, I've been placed in these situations far too often. They talk about sacrifices in parenting books all the time. It's the refrain of parenting: "It takes sacrifice." But no one ever really goes into the details. They give you some sort of watered-down *Leave It to Beaver* look at it, where a parent has to make some banal and yet slightly humorous decision. But no one ever, *ever* told me that I'd literally soak in nastiness all day, every day, until it became so ubiquitous that a stranger at Target would tell me there was something on my forearm and I'd realize that right there, on the skin, was a four-inch streak of dried toddler snot. I had no idea where it came from or how long it'd been there; yet until someone pointed it out, I was just living with it.

And no one told me that one day I'd be bleeding and splattered with dog pee and have to put all that on hold so I could wipe another human's butt.

I stood there for what seemed like an eternity, holding the cat above my head while the dog still lay on his back (although he wasn't peeing anymore), feeling a deep sense of being walked on.

"I'm done! Wipe! My! Butt!"

I put the cat in the garage. I turned around and noticed the dog had run off to hide somewhere in the house. His pee was still warm on my leg. Head bowed, shoulders slumped, feet dragging, I walked down the hall to wipe my daughter's butt.

Aspen sat smiling on the toilet, pink and yellow butterfly underwear around her ankles, legs kicking half a foot above the floor.

I'd gone to college. I'd written for the New York Times and the Washington Post. I worked at a major research university. I owned a mortgage and two cars. I had a solid credit score. How did I end up here?

I stood before the toilet, and she put her head down and to the side, her small arms hugging my leg. I reached in with my right hand and wiped her butt, my left hand against the wall for balance. It was one of those really nasty ones that required two or three passes with toilet paper and a wipe. As I worked, Aspen sang "You're Welcome" from *Moana* in the sweetest songbird voice.

I looked in the mirror above the sink and thought about how I'd gone to college. I'd written for the *New York Times* and the *Washington Post*. I worked at a major research university. I owned a mortgage and two cars. I had a solid credit score. How did I end up here?

I got Aspen settled. Then I tended to the mess in the kitchen. All of it before I cleaned myself and treated my own wounds.

I stood over the kitchen sink in a clean pair of shorts, bandages crisscrossing my arm, as I ate ice cream straight from the carton with a somber look on my face. From a distance, it probably looked like I'd just been dumped.

From behind, Aspen hugged me, her soft little arms around my knees.

I looked down. She looked up, blue eyes wide open, a smile on her face.

"Hold you'a me," she said.

I leaned down and picked her up and placed her on my hip. She reached out and ran her palm across my cheek in the sweetest way. She scanned my face, small blue eyes moving side to side. She smelled like graham crackers.

"What's this for?" I asked.

"I just love'a you," she said.

As nasty and picked on as I felt, it all washed away as I held her. Suddenly I felt a warm tenderness in my heart. I know this wasn't Aspen apologizing. But in the moment, it felt like she was trying to tell me something in her own three-year-old way. And for the sake of making myself feel better, I just assumed it was her telling me that, at the very least, she appreciated me.

"Thanks, kiddo," I said. "I love you too."

She leaned in and gave me a hug. Then she whispered into my ear, "I fart," and giggled.

Dad's Never
the Favorite

It was 7:45 p.m. on a Tuesday, and Mel and Norah were arguing. I was in the kitchen grading papers for my second job, and Mel was trying to get the kids to clean up and get ready for bed before their 8:00 bedtime. Tristan was cleaning his room. He was six. It's easier when they're six. But Norah was four and dressed in ballerina pajamas, her hair wet and combed. She was standing in the hallway, her arms folded in protest. Mel was in Christmas-tree pajama bottoms and an old T-shirt, standing in Norah's bedroom doorway, pointing.

Usually this was my job.

Generally, I came home from work, had dinner with the family, and then got the kids to bed while Mel did homework. She was in school at the time. But Tuesdays were different because they were the days that papers were due in the online classes I taught.

And I must say it made me feel a little better about my bedtime role to hear Mel struggle to get the kids to listen as much as I did. After all, she was the popular one.

Just a few days earlier, Norah received enough chore points to go out for ice cream. I asked her who she wanted to go with. Without hesitation, she said, "Mom."

"You know," I said, "I'll let you get more ice cream and toppings. The cone will be as big as your head. I'll let you pick the radio station. I might even slip you $100."

She stuck out her lip and said, "Mommy!"

I pulled the same exact move with Tristan a month earlier, and he picked Mommy too.

And sure, the $100 was an exaggeration. But even if it were real, I don't think Norah would have changed her mind. It could have been a million dollars and the deed to Cinderella's castle, and she'd still have picked her mother.

Norah always wanted to sit next to Mom while eating dinner or watching a movie. Sometimes she would say, without reason, "I only love Mommy!"

"But I love you too," I'd say.

Norah always, without hesitation, stomped her foot and yelled, "Only Mommy!"

I tried not to take stuff like this personally, but it was difficult. I wanted to be the popular one.

I wanted the kids to fight over me.

I wanted to go out for ice cream.

I wanted to live in Cinderella's castle.

Sometimes I wondered if the reason my kids loved Mel more than me was because of my nightly duty of getting them to clean up the living room and get ready for bed. On workdays, I had only one to two hours with my kids. And half of that time was spent yelling things like, "Stop screwing around in there and put soap on your body!"; "We just ate dinner, get out of the fridge!"; "Do you realize how fast this would go if you'd pick up more than one toy?"; and "I'm this close to putting you all up for adoption!" Basically, these were all the things my parents said, things I hated and swore I'd never say. And then—*bam!*—I'm in a work polo and pants from Costco and sounding exactly like my father.

Most days, I felt like all my kids heard was my angry-dad voice.

Basically, these were all the things my parents said, things I hated and swore I'd never say. And then—*bam!*—I'm in a work polo and pants from Costco and sounding exactly like my father.

In contrast, Mel got to have a healthy mix of angry frustrated-mom moments mixed with loving, fun, compassionate moments.

That night Mel was having a difficult time getting Norah to listen. Actually, I don't think "difficult" is a strong enough word. Perhaps I should say "horrible" or "hellish" or "light her hair on fire." You know what I'm talking about.

Norah's room, as usual, was an explosion of baby dolls wrapped in blankets. I'm not sure of the exact number of dolls Norah had, but I think it was somewhere between a million and infinity. And it was not always dolls she cared for. Her maternal instincts were epic. They reached out to stuffed animals, remote controls, fruit—really, anything that could be wrapped in a blanket. One day I found her swaddling a brown loafer in a *Hello Kitty* blanket, cooing, "You're just such a cutie! Now go to sleep."

Norah's room, as usual, was an explosion of baby dolls wrapped in blankets. I'm not sure of the exact number of dolls Norah had, but I think it was somewhere between a million and infinity.

I watched Mel from the hallway. She kept telling Norah to put the babies away, and Norah kept stomping her foot and yelling, "Shhh! The babies are sleeping!"

It was after 8:00 p.m. The two had already argued for nearly twenty minutes. Every time Mel went into Norah's room to try to clean things up, Norah screamed like a protective mother fighting off a kidnapper.

"Leave my babies alone!"

Both stood in the hallway. Mel folded her arms, looked our short little tyrant in the face, and said, "You know what? I'm giving you until the count of five to start cleaning. And if you don't, I'm putting all of your toys in boxes. Every one of them. All your babies! Your LEGOs! Your princess dresses! Everything!"

I must have used the "I'm going to count to five" tactic a million times—but like most parents, I'd get to five and run out of ideas, so I'd say something like, "Five and a half!"

Mel didn't yell all that often, so when she did, it was pretty stirring. It was low and raspy but not too loud—but it was loud enough. It wasn't exactly crazy, like she was experiencing an exorcism; it was somewhere just below that, where I could be pretty sure she was still of sound mind but I could also be confident that she could wield the power of the devil if required.

I must have used the "I'm going to count to five" tactic a million times—but like most parents, I'd get to five and run out of ideas, so I'd say something like, "Five and a half!" Then I'd raise my eyebrows so they knew I meant business. But the count-to-five tactic had about a 50 percent chance of working, and it was probably because my children had blown past five enough times to know I was bluffing.

However, I'd never gone as far as to say, "I'm going to take away all your toys." To someone who had easily gone past five time and time again, it seemed extreme.

Up until that moment, I'd still had half my concentration on grading papers. I leaned back from my laptop and gave the scene my full attention to see how it would play out. I assumed Norah would get busy, but before Mel had the opportunity to start counting, Norah said, "I don't care," in a bratty little voice, her head cocked to the side, voice snarky and entitled. "I'll just get more toys," she retorted.

Mel didn't argue.

She didn't count.

She didn't say a word.

She walked down the hall and through the kitchen, each step heavy and angry, into the garage. We had a bunch of boxes in the garage from when we'd moved (let's not talk about how long they'd been there). Mel came into the house with three large boxes and started packing up Norah's toys.

I assumed that Norah would step in, throw a fit, freak out, get me involved—something. But she didn't. She just sat on the sofa in the living room and watched. Her face was soft and calm, and I couldn't tell if she really thought we would buy her all new toys (which we wouldn't), or if she was just testing it all out, seeing what she could get away with.

I walked down the hall and stood in Norah's doorway.

"Do you really think this is a good idea?" I whispered. "It seems a bit extreme."

Mel put the final baby doll in a box full of baby dolls. She was hunched over the box, her brown hair falling into her face. She looked up at me with crazy blue-green eyes as she taped it shut.

"I'm sick of this crap. She needs to learn to pick up."

"Are you ever going to give them back?" I asked.

She didn't answer my question. She pushed the box toward me and said, "Take this to the garage."

As I hauled the box down the hallway and through the kitchen, all I could wonder was how this was all going to play out. What were the next few days going to be like? And then I had a selfish thought: *Perhaps this will make me Norah's favorite.*

Around noon the next day, I sent Mel a text. "How's Norah doing without toys? Does she hate you?"

I was hopeful when I sent that text.

Mel replied, "She's doing just fine. She hasn't had one fit this morning."

I was a little surprised by this response. It was my assumption that Norah, my sweet little Norah, was going to wake up, stretch her arms above her head, look around her room, realize all her babies were gone, and flip the eff out. In my mind, I saw her sprawled out on the floor, like I'd seen her do a million times, screaming and kicking and crying. I assumed that I'd get a text from Mel sometime midmorning, telling me she was ready to burn it all down.

But I got none of that.

Without her dolls, Norah was as good as a ticking, grumpy, fit-throwing toddler bomb.

It had to be just a matter of time, I thought. Without her dolls, Norah was as good as a ticking, grumpy, fit-throwing toddler bomb. Perhaps sometime in the afternoon I'd find out that Norah cracked, which caused Mel to crack. I had it all planned out: I'd come home from work to find Norah freaking out in her room. Mel would be in the kitchen, ready to put her head in the oven. And I would walk into the garage, grab Norah's boxes of toys, and solve the problem in a jolly-old-Saint-Nick sort of way.

And once Norah saw that I was the one who brought back her babies, she'd wrap her arms around me, lay a huge kiss on my cheek, and say, "I only love Daddy."

I'd be her favorite, no doubt about it.

I came home. The sofa wasn't lined with swaddled baby dolls like some low-budget production of *Annie*. Norah bounced around the living room in a pink T-shirt and leggings, obviously in a great mood.

She ran to the door and gave me a big hug. Then she waltzed into the living room and danced while humming to herself, not a toy in sight.

I looked at Mel, confused.

"She's been like this all day," Mel said. "It's the craziest thing. It makes me wish I'd taken her toys away a long time ago."

"Are you sure she doesn't hate you?" I asked.

Mel shrugged. "I almost get the impression she loves me more. She's been really snuggly today, and she keeps telling me that I'm a good mommy."

"Perhaps she's delusional with grief," I said.

"I can live with that if it means she's not screaming and I'm not picking up her crap every few minutes."

"This is nuts. You are always her favorite. *Always.* No matter what. I hate it."

Mel rolled her eyes and said, "This isn't a competition. Little kids just love their mothers best."

While I'd heard this several times, I never really understood what it meant until I was living it.

Then Mel winked and said, "Anyway, being second best can't be that bad."

"So you admit it," I said.

She shrugged, and I said, "We'll see about that, toy stealer."

While in the moment this all seemed playful, by that evening, it had started to itch, and I said something to Norah that wasn't all that mature. Or even edging on mature.

Later that night, when getting Norah ready for bed, I asked her to brush her teeth.

I assumed I'd gotten to her, and she was starting to realize that I was, indeed, the cool parent.

The better parent.

At least equal to, or maybe even better than, Mommy.

I might have just become the favorite.

I waited in anticipation.

Norah looked me in the face, eyes cold and flat, and cried, "Mommy! I only love Mommy!"

"I don't have to brush my teeth."

We argued. I chased her down the hall a few times. This was all standard. But what was unusual was that after I caught up with her and forced the toothbrush into her hand, she said, "You're just a mean daddy. I only love Mommy!"

"Really?" I asked. I gave her my straight-lipped serious face and said, "I'm not the one who took all your toys away."

She sat silently for a moment. She looked me in the face for some time, eyes narrowed, deep in thought. I assumed I'd gotten to her, and she was starting to realize that I was, indeed, the cool parent.

The better parent.

At least equal to, or maybe even better than, Mommy.

I might have just become the favorite.

I waited in anticipation.

Norah looked me in the face, eyes cold and flat, and cried, "Mommy! I only love Mommy!"

She stopped for a moment, fists at her sides, and screamed, "You're a mean daddy."

It was in that moment that I knew, without any doubt, that Mel could do anything to Norah and she'd still love her more than me. She could lock Norah in the attic and feed her nothing but dog food, or send her away to work on a boat full of hard labor and illness, or force her to watch nothing but educational TV, and she'd still draw pictures of Mel and her holding hands at the park, me far off in the distance with stink lines above my head.

Was I a mean dad? I didn't think so. Each night I read Norah a story. I got up with her in the night. I took her out on daddy-daughter dates. I let her comb my beard, as painful as that can be. She painted my nails once a week and told me how beautiful I was, even though I never felt all that beautiful when we were finished. I told her I loved her every day. But Mel? Her relationship with our four-year-old was unshakable.

A few moments later, Mel walked by and said, "Norah, please do what Daddy says."

She looked up at her mother, then at me, then placed the toothbrush in her mouth, eyeing me the whole time.

Mel didn't give Norah her toys back for over a week—mostly because she was so well behaved without them and the house was cleaner than it'd been since we moved in.

Norah also never once asked to have them back.

During that time, Norah didn't hold any resentment against her mother. And she still, like always, loved her more than me.

One day I came home from work, and the living room was filled with swaddled babies again. I asked Mel why she gave them back, and she said, "I was starting to feel guilty. Norah's been really sweet the past week. She's obviously earned them back. So we went into the garage and brought her toys out."

Mel told me that Norah didn't seem surprised, even after Mel reminded her of the missing baby dolls. She acted like she didn't remember any of it. This was one of the reasons parenting our four-year-old was so frustrating. She remembered only about half of what I told her, and most of what she did remember had to do with her asking to go to Chuck E. Cheese, and my saying "maybe," and then her acting like it was a blood oath.

But sometimes, with a little prompting, she did remember the important things.

I went into the living room, and Norah was cradling a stuffed puppy she'd wrapped in a blanket. I didn't say anything about her getting her dolls back, and I didn't remind her who took them away. I didn't pull any of those old moves in a vain attempt to be her favorite.

Instead I asked, "What's your baby's name?"

Norah thought for a moment. She was holding the swaddled stuffed puppy in one hand. And as she thought, she mindlessly rubbed her other hand against her blue puffy dress.

"DJ Lance Rock," she said.

"Wow!" I said. "What a beautiful name."

"This is my favorite baby," she said.

"Do you know who gave you that stuffed puppy?" I asked.

Norah thought about it for a moment, and said, "Nope."

"It was me. I brought it home for you after my trip to Washington, DC. I saw it in a store and thought, *Norah would love that because she loves puppies.* So I bought it for you."

Norah smiled. "I do remember." Then she dropped the stuffed puppy and jumped into my chest and wrapped her arms around my neck, almost pushing me over.

"You're just a cute daddy," she said. "The best daddy."

I thought about Mel taking away Norah's toys and how it didn't faze Norah. I thought about how Mel will most likely always be Norah's favorite. But as she hugged me, I realized it wasn't really about that. It was about having a relationship with my daughter, and it was about making sure she knew I loved her.

I didn't say anything.

I just let her give me a big hug.

Face It—
You'll Never
Pee Alone

We stopped at a gas station in middle-of-nowhere Oregon, two hours into a twelve-hour road trip to a family funeral, when the diarrhea struck. Mel and the two older kids were in the van, while I was inside looking for cornflakes with our four-year-old, Aspen.

We beelined into the restroom, my left hand holding Aspen's hand as I tugged her along and she drug behind, pointing and asking for everything she saw along the way. My right hand was holding my cheeks, my butt was clenched, my steps awkward. I threw open the stall door, pushed Aspen in with me, placed her in the corner, shut the door, locked it, and dropped my pants. Aspen watched as I struggled, her *Moana* light-up Crocs on the wrong feet, blue eyes wide and supportive, hands clapping. "Good job, Daddy! Good job! You make two poops! Now three poops! I'm four!"

"Yucky, Daddy. It's stinky."

We made eye contact for a moment. She smiled at me.

I didn't smile back.

Instead I thought about the fact that her watching me do my business had become more or less as normal as a sink and a mirror in a restroom.

The night before we left for our trip, I was about to lock the restroom door when Aspen shoved her light-up Minnie Mouse shoe in the way. She pushed her little blonde head in and said, "I just come in with you, Daddy."

I tried to fight her, like I always did. I pushed her out, and she pushed with everything she had to get in, and I knew I had two choices: (1) I could let her watch, or (2) I could listen to her scream and bang at the door like she had a warrant for my arrest.

I let her in, like I often did, and had the pleasure of listening to her scream at me to "sit down" and that I was "doing it wrong." She pushed at the back of my knees, and I struggled to keep my balance while trying to fight her off with my left hand, pee splashing out of the bowl several times.

Not that every time she entered it was this exciting. Mostly she just stood and silently watched me, her eyes all inquisitive and creepy, like Michael Myers watching one of his future murder victims. Or she'd ask to sit on my lap if it were a number two, as if that's normal . . .

or comfortable. Sometimes she barged in, string cheese in hand, and watched me while she ate, as though she'd snuck her own snacks into a movie.

All of it was awkward.

Mostly she just stood and silently watched me, her eyes all inquisitive and creepy, like Michael Myers watching one of his future murder victims. Or she'd ask to sit on my lap if it were a number two, as if that's normal . . . or comfortable.

I don't know if toddlers have always watched their parents do their business. Perhaps it's been the case since forever. Perhaps Cain and Abel watched Eve. Who knows? Maybe it's just my generation. I mean, honestly, a moment of peace? With a four-year-old? Forget about it.

I longed to pee alone.

There was something different about that moment at the gas station, though, and it had little to do with Aspen watching me and everything to do with how supportive she was being.

I'm not sure what happened exactly—if I'd eaten something bad or if it was the stress of traveling with kids to a funeral, but what I do know is that my four-year-old was the Richard Simmons of pooping. I'd never felt so supported in anything in my whole life. She commented on the size, smell, and sound: "Wow!" She commented on my work ethic: "You're trying so hard!" At one point, I had to push her face away from the business end of things as she clapped and cried, "You're doing it, Daddy! You're doing it!"

In the past two months, we'd been extra supportive of her endeavors to pee in the potty. Not that we hadn't always been supportive. We got all excited when she first started going, but there was a point when she refused to go—she avoided it and fought it and walked into the restroom with her arms hanging at her sides as if using the restroom were some sort of chore and peeing her pants was a right we were denying her.

"You're trying so hard!" At one point, I had to push her face away from the business end of things as she clapped and cried, "You're doing it, Daddy! You're doing it!"

So we went from supportive to punitive. We took away screen time when she had an accident. We took away treats and toys. We gave her some time-outs. Well, it backfired. She started to associate using the restroom with punishment and began hiding her soiled underwear around the house whenever she had an accident. I found peed-in underwear tucked behind her bed, stashed behind her bedroom door, and rotting in the toy box. Her favorite tactic was to wrap a number two mishap in a wad of clothing and stuff it in the bottom of the laundry basket.

The smell in my house was legendary. I felt like I spent most of my evenings sniffing out clues, always on the search for some accident Aspen was hiding.

This all came to a head one afternoon when I was home sick from work and accidentally put a turd in the dryer. I put some laundry in the dryer that I assumed was clean—but it wasn't.

I'd love to blame it all on the fever I was battling. I didn't think for a moment to check that load in the washer for an additional load. I can't even remember if the laundry felt wet. For all I know, Mel might have put some laundry in the washer, forgot to start it, and then I came along like the world's biggest idiot and tossed it all in the dryer, assuming that I was pitching in. But I was actually baking a turd buried somewhere in a pair of *Peppa Pig* underwear.

But the smell of baked toddler poop lingered.

I didn't realize what happened until Mel woke me from a nap for an interrogation. It took a while for my face to go red. She'd already taken the dirty clothing out of the dryer, found the crispy turd, thrown it out, and put the clothing back in the washer, hopeful that it'd come clean.

But the smell of baked toddler poop lingered.

I'm not sure how long it stayed in there, heating up and tumbling around, but the smell was something I'd never experienced before: a mix of dryer lint, fabric sheets, burning rubber, and, well, poop. Black turd skids lined the inside of the dryer. I wiped it down. Disinfected it. I felt faint from my cold and nauseous from the smell. I expended a good amount of elbow grease to get the dryer clean, all the while praying I wouldn't have to buy a new wardrobe for my toddler (along with a new dryer).

It was then that I knew something had to change. So instead of being punitive, instead of getting frustrated and angry with Aspen each time she slipped up and went in her pants, I started being extra, super, over-the-top enthusiastic whenever she used the restroom.

I clapped and said supportive things like, "Good job, Aspen, good job," and, "You're trying so hard!"

I even tried to make a game of it by counting her poops.

And while that change in strategy had come together nicely (she'd been on a serious roll when it came to not missing the toilet), she'd obviously gotten used to the positive reinforcement.

When I was cheering her on in our family restroom, it seemed normal, even appropriate. But when the roles were reversed, it was just, well, awkward. Particularly in a public restroom where the man in the stall next to me was obviously holding back tears of laughter—laughter that burst loose when Aspen called me a "pooping, farting robot."

Silence Is a Scary Sound

It all passed, and as I buckled
Aspen into the car seat, holding a
small package of antidiarrheal pills in my
mouth, Mel asked what took so long.
I looked at the ground and mumbled,
"You don't want to know."

Then she smiled and clapped some more, and I realized that despite this being one of the most embarrassing moments of my life, it was obvious that Aspen appreciated my efforts to teach her to use the restroom because mimicry is the best form of flattery.

Or at least, that's what I've heard.

It all passed, and as I buckled Aspen into the car seat, holding a small package of antidiarrheal pills in my mouth, Mel asked what took so long. I looked at the ground and mumbled, "You don't want to know."

It was then that Aspen was kind enough to recount the story to her mother, clapping the whole time.

"Daddy did a good job!" she said. Then she held up all ten of her fingers and said, "He pooped this many times!"

I was in the driver's seat, buckling my seat belt, watching Aspen in the rearview mirror. Mel patted my leg and said, "Nice work, Daddy."

All I could do was say, "Thank you."

You Will Freak Out over Spilled Juice— Be Sure to Apologize

Aspen spilled half a jug of juice on the table, chairs, floor, and, well . . . she basically made it rain in the kitchen. If you know anything about four-year-olds, you know their power to spill is on par with the Infinity Gauntlet.

You assume I'm exaggerating, which is an easy thing to do because if you've made it this far in the book, you already know that I often exaggerate. I wish I were, but this time I. Am. Not.

Apple juice coated the table, the chair and all its crevices, the wall, the floor, Aspen, and several other items. All of it was sticky.

And to make it worse, this wasn't the first time she'd made a mess with juice, or milk, or any number of other liquids. I used to watch scary movies. Now I just watched my four-year-old handle liquid without a lid. Some of you reading this are rolling your eyes and being all, "Why don't you only give her liquid with a lid?"

Let me tell you something. At this time, there were a number of cool things in my house. Princess Twilight Sparkle was cool. Putting shoes on your hands was cool. Jumping from the couch to the easy chair was cool. Face paint was cool.

Lids on cups were *not* cool. The last thing Aspen wanted was a lid. She also insisted on a "big-kid plate" at dinner then overfilled it and ate only two bites. And she always wanted to open her own bags of chips, which she always did open—I'll give her that—but she never did it gracefully. She opened them like she were a T-Rex. I could drive to the moon in the time it took her to buckle her seat belt, and I could walk a marathon in the time it took her to put on shoes.

Her motto was "I do it myself," regardless of where we needed to be and regardless of whether I'd just cleaned the house.

I wanted her to be independent. I wanted her to grow up and learn how to handle things for herself. I wanted her to pay her own bills, pick her own battles, find her own political party, and be willing to look a boss in the face and let them know she wanted a raise. I wanted her to break the glass ceiling. I wanted her to become a nuclear engineer, or the president, or the only female president who was also a nuclear engineer and fought crime at night with nuclear technology. I wanted her to be all of those things and more, but the moment she wanted to buckle her own seat belt when we were already running late for a doctor's appointment, it took every ounce of my strength to stand there for the seconds that felt like hours, watching her fight to do something simple, and not shove her little hands out of the way and buckle it myself.

This was one of my biggest struggles. I wanted her to become more independent, but I found it really difficult to take my hands off the wheel and allow her time to be independent.

Not that we were going anywhere during that particular spill.

The real stress was that we'd just bought a new house in a much nicer neighborhood, and the only reason we could afford it was because the place needed some remodeling. Not that we had to strip the place down to its studs, but I did rip out most of the carpet, some floorboards, and some drywall, and I painted.

When we bought the house, Mel and I were stupid enough to assume that we could do all this work ourselves while living there, and it would be amazing, and the house would one day look like St. Paul's Cathedral. But if you could actually see my hands right now, you'd notice how soft and tender they are, without anything resembling a callus. I type for a living. I changed my own oil once and I was like, "That sucked. I'm never doing that again." Last year I called AAA because I removed all the lug nuts from my flat tire and still couldn't get the stupid thing off. I can't turn a screw without cross-threading it, and the weekend before the juice spill I had to get a tetanus shot, lost a toenail, and almost cried because I threw out my back.

I'm not a handy guy.

It's a fact.

> I type for a living. I changed my own oil once and I was like, "That sucked. I'm never doing that again."

All those home repairs were stressing me out, and I was tired of ripping things apart only to find rot, or bugs, or a dead bird and having to do more work when I was already working two jobs on top of remodeling a house.

Then, to make it all sting just a little more, I had mopped the dining room thirty minutes before the apple juice spill.

Okay. Wait.

That's not true.

I didn't mop. Tristan did. A fact that makes me sound like I'm complaining just for the sake of complaining . . .

But!

I argued with him for twenty minutes to do it, then helped move the table and chairs and fill the mop bucket. So outside of the act of moving the mop, I'd mopped.

And I hate mopping. If I had to pick between mopping and slamming my head in a car door, I'd take the car door—so the thought of mopping twice in one day felt like two car doors, and I just wasn't up for that kind of punishment.

What had I done to deserve this? Nothing. No parent ever does.

I came downstairs, I saw the mess, and I flipped.

I'd been upstairs painting a closet. I had a headache from the fumes. Tristan was supposed to be watching his sister, but he was too "focused" on his Rubik's cube to notice her reenacting a scene from *Titanic* with apple juice in the kitchen. I said all the parenting clichés: "What were you thinking?" and "You are both going to your rooms!" and "I don't have time for another mess!"

Tristan said he was sorry.

Aspen started to cry.

Then I noticed something.

On the floor, under the table, were two dishrags soaking up juice.

In Aspen's hand was another.

"Were you trying to clean up your mess?" I asked.

Aspen gave the saddest, most tearful nod I'd ever seen, her lower lip quivering.

And—*poof!*—just like that, I felt low.

Very low.

There was no way she could've cleaned the mess herself. She did create more work for me when I already had a bunch of remodeling work to do that day. But none of that was important.

She'd tried to pour herself a glass of juice, spilled it, and now she was attempting to clean it up.

Everything she did was exactly what I'd been trying to teach her about being an independent human. I'm not supposed to cry over spilled milk (or, in this case, juice), but it happens. I think most parents have done it a time or two. I get so caught up in the mess, and the work, and the "one more thing to do" that I don't pause for a moment to see what's *really* happening.

I crouched down and said, "I'm sorry, kiddo. I overreacted." I gave her a hug.

Once we'd both calmed down, I got the mop out again. I moved the chairs again. And together, Aspen and I cleaned up the mess. It probably took fifteen minutes, tops.

Then I sat next to Aspen at the table, got the juice back out, and watched her carefully pour another glass.

She took a long drink, then she looked over at me with a sly dimpled grin and said, "It's cool, Daddy. It's cool."

I don't know where she picked up that phrase, but she'd been saying it a lot. I couldn't help but laugh. Then I put my arm around her and said, "Yeah. It's cool."

She leaned across her chair to crawl into my lap, and as she did, she pushed a saltshaker onto the floor. It smashed open, making another mess.

I stood and went for the broom. Under my breath, I whispered, "It's cool, Daddy. It's cool."

When It's Your Last, You Can't Help but Play Favorites

Once the water was above my waist, I looked at Mel, who was sitting comfortably on a beach chair, a book in her lap. I mouthed, "It's so cold. I hate you right now."

She blew me a kiss.

We were in the Oregon mountains, renting a house for the weekend, which was part of a homeowner's association with a pool. My wife, who conveniently "forgot" her swimming suit (well played, Mel) told our children—most importantly, our four-year-old—that we could go swimming.

According to the thermostat on the van, it was fifty-five degrees. That was in the sun. The pool was in the shade. The owner of the house said the pool was heated, but, unless she was from Siberia, she lied. For me, a thirty-something father of three used to Oregon weather, each step deeper, each splash, each ripple felt like Alaska.

The tall teenager checking people into the clubhouse was in a hoodie and long pants. As we had walked past him, he had a somber look on his face that seemed to say, "Are you sure about this?" There were three people in the pool when we arrived: two skinny, freckle-faced kids with chattering teeth and some gray-haired lady swimming laps as comfortably as a polar bear.

Before we hit the pool, I made suggestions. I said we could play hide-and-seek in the rental house. I said we could go for another hike.

I even offered ice cream.

It didn't matter.

There was no changing their minds.

But to be truthful, it wasn't the older two children that really pushed me to get into that pool. Over the years, I've told them "no" to a million things, a million times. It was Aspen, my four-year-old, my last and youngest child, in her little red, white, and blue Popsicle swimming suit and purple armband life preservers, who ultimately got me into the pool. It was her bright blue eyes and blonde pigtails tugging at my every instinct to make her happy. It was her excited dance, her flapping arms, and the way she lit up the moment swimming was mentioned.

Everything about her, from head to toe, was more excited than I'd ever been in my whole life, and I knew without a doubt that if I turned her down, I'd never hear the end of it, because when you're four, swimming is a huge deal. Every day when I came home from work, regardless of the season, Aspen was in a swimming suit, goggles attached to her forehead. Sometimes I just filled the bathtub and let her splash around because I knew it was the only way to keep her from asking to go swimming over and over again, as if we had nothing better to do than drop everything and take that little girl to the pool

Everything about her, from head to toe, was more excited than I'd ever been in my whole life, and I knew without a doubt that if I turned her down, I'd never hear the end of it, because when you're four, swimming is a huge deal.

Mel went to great lengths to hide Aspen's swimming suits to keep her from insisting on wearing them to daycare, or to church, or to the store, or outside in a snowstorm. When she knew there was a pool available, there was no changing her mind. The pool could be 55 percent urine. It could have a glacier. It could have the man-eating fish dinosaur from *Jurassic World* waiting for a hot meal. We were going swimming.

I'd told my older two children "no" to swimming in a freezing pool more than once while on vacation, but I don't think I'd ever said "no" to swimming while on vacation with Aspen.

Don't get me wrong—I was comfortable with my decision to end my child-making days, but it did make me pretty sentimental.

She was my youngest. As far as I was concerned, she was my last. I'd gotten a vasectomy about a year after her birth, and while I wasn't all that keen on getting the procedure done—most men aren't—I did it because my wife had handled the heavy lifting of birth control for long enough, and it was time for me to step up. But what I didn't realize was that once the swelling went down and it was confirmed that my seed was zero, I would start to look at my youngest and realize that I wasn't going to have any more children and that I needed to jump on every moment.

Don't get me wrong—I was comfortable with my decision to end my child-making days, but it did make me pretty sentimental.

A week before our trip to the cabin, Aspen fell while running to the playground, scuffed her knee, and cried. So I swept her up into my arms and carried her back to the van, her head buried in my chest, her body all tears and boogers and heavy breathing, and all I could think about was how many of these moments we had left.

I hated that she was hurt, sure, but there's something so wonderful about having my littlest one cling to me with her arms around my neck, crying into my chest, clearly knowing that I was the source of all comfort and protection.

During that moment, I had a lot of questions: How much longer would my kisses mean something? How much longer would she be small enough to be carried, and how much longer would she allow me to carry her?

As I tended to Aspen's knee, I tried to remember the last time Tristan and Norah needed help with a cut, or needed to be carried or kissed, or allowed me to hug them in front of their friends. And I couldn't. It happened so gradually; yet it happened, and there I was, wishing I could get those little people back and knowing that it was happening with Aspen, right there, right then. So I gave her an extra kiss and carried her back to the playground even though she didn't need me to, savoring that tender moment.

As crazy as it sounds, I had a similar warm feeling holding Aspen in that freezing swimming pool.

Was I playing favorites?

Gosh, I don't know. Maybe? But I don't really think so. It was more about my being just a little more sentimental in my midthirties combined with my knowing that Aspen was my last and the simple power of her being an adorable little kid that made me more willing to do some uncomfortable things I wouldn't normally do.

Aspen laughed and splashed me.

I cringed. She hung from me. I caught her as she jumped from the side of the pool, each time dreading the moment her body hit the water because I knew it would throw a freezing splash into my face. I looked over at Mel, snug in her jacket and dry pants. Sometimes she winked at me, but mostly she buried her nose in her warm and dry book.

I glared at her.

At one point I looked at Aspen, and her lips matched her blue swimming suit and her skin tight across her body, and I said, "You're freezing."

She shook her head and said, "No, I not." Then she splashed me in the face again.

Once it was all said and done and I'd dragged Aspen out of the clubhouse kicking and screaming, I knew that by the time I got all the kids bathed and it was my turn for a shower, we'd be out of hot water. I don't know how long we spent in that pool. Twenty minutes? Thirty minutes? A lifetime?

After bath time, as I tucked Aspen into bed, I asked if she'd had fun on our vacation. She smiled and nodded. And when I asked what her favorite part was, she didn't mention the hike. She didn't mention our drive or all the amazing animals we saw. She didn't even mention our trip to McDonald's for lunch. All she talked about was the pool, about how awesome it was. How much fun she'd had, and how she wanted to go back first thing in the morning before we left to go home.

"Yeah," I said with a hesitant laugh. "Maybe . . ."

Once a Child Can Turn On the TV in the Morning, Your Life Begins Again

I woke up at 9:00 a.m. on a Saturday to the sound of *Moana* playing on the TV. All three of our children, even Aspen, the youngest, had been up for who knows how long. None of them had come into our room to ask for a snack, or to tattle on the other, or to inform me of the simple and irritating truth that they were awake. Mel was still asleep, probably catching up on ten years of not being able to sleep past 5:30 a.m., while I gazed at the ceiling.

We were in this exhausting stage, waiting on Aspen, our little caboose, to stop wandering into our room at the crack of dawn. We were waiting for our son and daughter, ten and seven years old, both very capable of getting up in the morning and caring for themselves, to follow my guidance on getting Aspen breakfast and putting a movie on the TV so Mel and I could sleep in a little on the weekends. Not that they cared about our sleep, or our well-being, or our general mental health.

I don't want to speak for all parents here, but sleep was the most coveted item in our house. Mel and I were always negotiating with each other for more, so to have our children get up and manage themselves on a Saturday morning was basically manna from heaven.

It felt like we were waiting for an endless assortment of gears to shift so that Mel and I wouldn't have to spend Saturday mornings sleeping in shifts, one of us getting up early—earlier than I realized early could be—while the other slept, then swapping at about 8:00 a.m. and letting the other go back to bed, making it so both of us weren't fully up and going until almost noon and leaving little to zero time to clean our wreck of a house, both of us only moderately rested.

I don't want to speak for all parents here, but sleep was the most coveted item in our house. Mel and I were always negotiating with each other for more, so to have our children get up and manage themselves on a Saturday morning was basically manna from heaven.

It was better than finishing college, or a huge raise at work, or sex, or winning the lottery.

And on this Saturday, it finally happened.

I rolled over to look at Mel. She was facing me. Her eyes opened, but she quickly squinted, not sure what to make of the sunlight peeking into our bedroom. Both of us were far too used to being woken before dawn.

"What time is it?" she asked. It felt like she was asking what year it was. It felt like we'd fallen into a time wrinkle, taking us back to the years before we had children. Back to when we used to complain about being tired because we'd accidentally slept too much. Back to when getting up before 9:00 a.m. felt like a real sacrifice.

Before children, I'd gone a few nights in a row with little sleep. I'd burned the candle at both ends for school, or for parties, or simply to watch back-to-back movies. But with kids, there really is no slowing down. There is no catch-up-on-sleep day. Sometimes I think about all the sleep I wasted before children and I want to punch myself in the face. I just didn't realize what I had.

Each child we had upped the ante, making it all snowball by creating more nighttime distractions. One kid might go to bed early, while another decided to fight it with every inch of their little body. Then once they were all asleep, the third decided to wet the bed. And all of them, every single one, regardless of what time we put them to bed, were up before daylight.

And it wasn't a few days of this, or a week, or even a month.

It was years.

Years of sleepless nights followed by early mornings until I was exhausted, caffeinated, redacted, and cut down to a fraction of who I was before kids. I forgot what it felt like to be rested, how to not drift off at work, while watching a movie, at stoplights.

Every single one, regardless of what time we put them to bed, were up before daylight. And it wasn't a few days of this, or a week, or even a month.

It was years.

I smiled at Mel.

"It's 9:05," I said.

Mel opened her eyes wider. Then she rolled onto her back and just lay there, speechless.

"This is the best moment of my life," Mel said.

She reached beneath the blankets and took my hand.

I didn't say anything.

I just breathed it in. We rested there for a couple more minutes, neither of us speaking, enjoying our bed for the first time in a long time.

I rolled over and kissed her lips. Then I moved

down to her neck, and I thought maybe, just maybe, it might happen this morning. Something that hadn't happened in the morning for a very long time.

I'm not sure where she found the chocolate. I'm not sure who gave it to her. I knew that it was smeared somewhere in the house, probably on the easy chair, the only decent piece of furniture we owned.

It was then that Aspen crept into our room.

Her face was smeared with chocolate. It dripped down her neck and onto the front of her baby-blue *Peppa Pig* nightgown. It was mashed into her blonde hair. She smiled up at us, and her teeth were spackled with it.

I'm not sure where she found the chocolate. I'm not sure who gave it to her. I knew that it was smeared somewhere in the house, probably on the easy chair, the only decent piece of furniture we owned.

I finally understood why she'd let us sleep so long, but I didn't care.

I was grateful that it'd finally happened, and I was optimistic that it would happen again.

I'd never been so optimistic about this whole parenting gig than I was after sleeping in until 9:00 a.m. on a Saturday.

I felt like a real person again.

It's amazing what a good night's rest can do.

Aspen tried to climb into our bed, but Mel stopped her before she got chocolate on the bedding. Then Mel picked Aspen up from behind, Aspen's chocolate-covered hands reaching out, and carried her into the bathroom to wash up.

I sat on the end of the bed and stretched, and as I did, I heard Mel say, "Thank you for letting us sleep."

Aspen giggled.

I asked her who turned on the TV, and she told me it was her brother.

I looked at my wife and winked.

Then I went into the living room to find a delightful mess. As a parent, I often say I'd do anything for my children. But deep down inside, I'd actually do anything for more sleep. I think most parents secretly feel this way. So you know what—that chocolate mess? It was totally worth it.

And hey, at least it wasn't poop.

Acknowledgments

In my last book, I thanked a lot of people. But with this one, I'd like to thank only one person. Mel: When we first met, I was twenty-one and working full-time at a hardware store. I told you I wanted to go to college, but I didn't know how to type, and I'd never read a novel, and I'd been out of high school for years, and I honestly didn't know where to start. You didn't run away. You didn't see me as some sad, pathetic, go-nowhere chump (which I was). All you said was, "Don't worry. I'll help you." During that first semester, I handwrote all my papers. My handwriting and spelling were so poor you couldn't read them, so I'd sit next to you in that dumpy, one-bedroom, across-the-street-from-the-liquor-store apartment of yours and read my papers aloud as you hunched over a keyboard and typed.

That arrangement of my handwriting my papers and your typing them stopped after one semester, once I learned how to type. But you helping me, well, that never stopped. You proofread millions of drafts. You pulled me up when I was low and frustrated and couldn't for the life of me figure out how I was ever going to make it as a writer. You left your family and friends in Utah to follow me to Minnesota for an MFA in creative writing and then to Oregon for my first big-kid, after-college job. You gave me three of the most wonderful people in the world, our children. You helped me figure out Blogger so I could put up that first blog post, and you allowed me to write openly about our marriage and our children.

You are the most wonderful person in this world, and my life, the father I am now, the person I have become, this book, the book before it, and the books I will write after it wouldn't have been possible if you hadn't stuck to that simple promise you made all those years ago: "Don't worry. I'll help you."

About the Author

Clint Edwards is the author of the hilarious collection of apologies to his wife and children, *I'm Sorry . . . Love, Your Husband* and creator of the funny and insightful daddy blog No Idea What I'm Doing. He is a staff writer for the very popular (and awesome) Scary Mommy and a parenting contributor to the *New York Times*, the *Washington Post*, *Huffington Post*, and other publications.

Clint's Index

All the times I mention poop: Stories on pages 14, 17–19, 41, 43–49, 54, 55, 71–75, 78, 82, 103, 111, 143, 145–147, 158, 159, 168, 182, 195, 226, 227, 231–233, 236–238, 255, 257, 259–261, 284

Times my toddlers embarrassed me in church: Stories on pages 23, 71

Every time Mel has considered divorce and/or murdering me: Stories on pages 1–288

My trips to the hospital: Stories on pages 33, 149

Times I've called the fire department: Story on page 87

Times I was given heartfelt parenting advice from a stranger: Stories on pages 65, 123, 149

Unexpected toddler nudity: Stories on pages 41, 65

Every time I have checked my toddler's symptoms on WebMD and it backfired: Stories on pages 33, 163

Each time I assumed my children were permanently damaged physically/emotionally: Stories on pages 51, 123, 255, 271

Nasty smells: Stories on pages 41, 59, 109, 231, 255

Fits/meltdowns (parents included): Stories on pages 157, 189, 201, 213

Places that have banned my toddlers for life: Stories on pages 99, 189, 201

Sex: (not found)

Sanity: (not found)

Sleep: (not found)

Hope: Story on page 279